Creative display

Ron Adams

Stanley Thornes (Publishers) Ltd

Introduction

This book aims to provide you with a huge bank of visual inspiration, ideas and techniques for display work in your class and school. It contains more than 90 thematic displays plus a section at the front on useful display techniques which are used throughout the book.

All the displays have been created with children in authentic classroom situations and have arisen out of ongoing class work. The displays fall loosely into thematic groups. For example the first few displays relate to the theme of Our World, move on to Ourselves, then Homes and so on. We have not explicitly labelled the displays by theme but have set them together on the contents page opposite to indicate thematic sections.

A rich display will stimulate a wide range of structured curriculum work; throughout we have provided linking ideas for subject work. Each subject is designated by a simple logo; you will see these set out below. 'Try these' sections provide further ideas.

Most of the displays and ideas can be interpreted widely across the 5-11 age range, although a few are aimed more narrowly. For example, 'We've arrived' is intended for children starting school for the first time.

Displays can have many different functions in a class and school. They can showcase children's work, present the school to visitors, provide information or inspiration, start a project or summarize it, or simply delight with rich visual effects and colours. All types of display are presented here, but our aim throughout has been to provide the inspiration for creating bright, lively, stimulating environments in which children can learn and grow.

Acknowledgements

The author and publisher would like to thank the children and staff of the following Wiltshire schools for their generous help in making this book possible:
Westlea CP, Swindon (Head Neil Griffiths), Windmill Hill CP, Swindon (Head Dave Messenger and Deputy Mark Hazzard), Walwayne Court CP, (Head Richard Brown), Winsley CE Primary, (Head Lawson Pratt and Deputy Head Pauline Knight), Box Highlands (Head Mike Plummer), Sutton Veny CE Primary (Head Christine Folker).
Thanks are also due to The Director of the Wiltshire Library & Museum Service and John Murphy, Deputy Head of St. Stephen's CE Primary, Bath.

All paper and card supplied by Slater Harrison and Co. Ltd. from their 'tailor made for schools' range of products. For details: Alan Deery 01625 573155.

Subject Logos

Geography | History | Science | RE | Music | Maths | English | Design and Technology | Art

Contents

Techniques for display

Classroom displays

Display & your school

First impressions

Welcome to our school

Visitors to schools are immediately given an impression of the style, approach and success of the school by the way it looks. A major part of this impression is given by the way display is used throughout the school. Teachers have to use their time more and more efficiently, while making the best and most imaginative use of space for practical work, reading and display.

Entrance halls

Displays in entrance halls are particularly important as they give the first impression that visitors get of your school. Even the most awkward spaces that can be found in entrance halls need to be used effectively and imaginatively. The drawing on page 39 shows how an unusual corner has been used to present a three dimensional display of *Jack and the Beanstalk*.

Difficult places

Transform concrete walls by using painted shelves on which can be mounted artwork and artefacts in matching colours. Corners in offices can be fitted with arrangements of dried flowers or/and children's pictures mounted on marbled paper. Room dividing shelves can host changing, seasonal or craft displays such as the Noah's ark below.

Wonderful things

A really attractive and comprehensive picture of the activities in your school can easily be presented as shown above. Collect examples of work from all ages, mount them in a varied and interesting way.

Mix double and triple mounted flat artwork with small three dimensional pieces and a happy cloud shaped title. It is important to have examples of all children's work on a rotating basis.

A friendly classroom

Children need to feel at home in their classroom. Values of caring for each other and the environment can be stimulated or stunted, to some extent, in stimulating or sterile classrooms. If children see you taking care they are more likely to be caring themselves. Make your classroom friendly.

The photograph (right) shows a quiet reading area surrounded by books (some of which the children have made) and provided with some cushions and a comfortable little chair enriched by an imaginative approach to the use of wall space and ceilings. Scrolls have been tied at the start of a timeline that wanders all across the ceiling to attract the attention during the day. A corner wall display combines artefacts and beautifully made miniature worlds that children have planned and constructed. This sort of mixture can bring liveliness and be a continuous source of interest. The appropriate use of resources improves the quality of education.

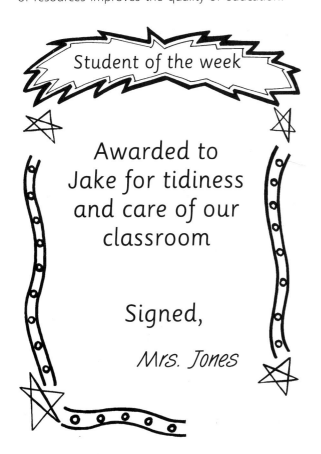

Student of the week

Awarded to
Jake for tidiness
and care of our
classroom

Signed,

Mrs. Jones

The photograph (above) shows how materials and resources when kept tidy and in order add a pleasant atmosphere to the classroom. Children love organising things and this activity could be part of a class points system. At the end of the week, award a student of the week certificate.

Display boards

Using display boards

Free standing boards

These can be used in the following ways:

- As room dividers (three or four sections). This can assist with floor planning.
- L and U shaped features.
- To provide shelving units (for work sheets).
- To emphasise titles by using header sections.
- As part of desk top displays.
- To make the best use of lighting.

Covering boards

Hessian and Expoloop are fabrics which can be used to cover display boards. Hessian can look dated and still requires pins or staples to mount work. Of the two, Expoloop offers substantial advantages:

- It comes in a variety of colours.
- It looks soft, friendly and modern.
- Easy to use to upgrade or create display boards.
- Extremely easy to mount on using Velcro.

Making your own boards

Transforming boards with Expoloop

1 Select the colour for the boards. This may vary according to location. Remove edging strips and clean.
2 Clean surface, lightly rub down with sandpaper.
3 Measure and cut Expoloop fabric to fit.
4 Apply adhesive to the boards (one at a time) either with paint sponge roller or special applicator.
5 Fix fabric to board, accurately smoothing as you go (like wallpapering).
6 Once dry, refit repainted edging strip.

Once the boards have been covered allow them to dry. Artwork and small artefacts can be mounted using Velcro adhesive strips. Adhesive Velcro is also available as *dots* and *dashes* (ready cut pieces). Staples, pins and other methods of fixing are no longer necessary.(Expoloop from Marler Haley)

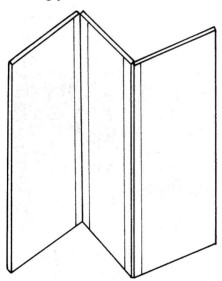

Fix inside faces first.

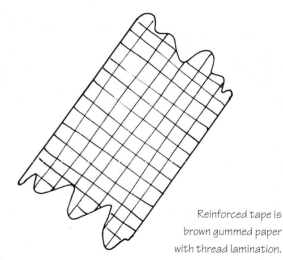

Reinforced tape is brown gummed paper with thread lamination.

Strong and attractive display boards can be made from heavy duty board called Tri-wall (available from Controlled Packaging of Westbury, Wiltshire). A simple free standing unit starts with three pieces of board the same size. Cut four pieces of fabric reinforced gum tape the height of the boards. Place two boards face to face as shown ensuring that the edges are perfectly in line. Use one piece of tape and secure as shown. When dry, open to 90 degrees and use another piece of tape to fix the inside faces. Complete for the three boards. The boards can be painted in any colour. As an alternative to paint you can use Expoloop or paper backed hessian on all surfaces.

Resources

Fabric reinforced gum, borders, table, pins, corrugated card and tape, Selotape, Copydex, Expoloop, Tri-wall boards, Velcro

Corrugated card

Versatile and colourful

Where to get it

Corrugated card (paper) comes in giant rolls (1.95 metres by 20 metres) in the following colours: black, grey, blue, red, primrose, green and white. It is available from NES Arnold and some LEAs. This versatile material can be used in a number of ways.

Mini displays

Use a small table (squared or circular) and fix a cut piece of corrugated card to go about three quarters of the way around the table. The card can be simply fixed around the edge using Blutack at regular close intervals. If you use a piece of wood instead of table then you can use a staple gun. The surface can then be dressed in fabric or in colour coordinated craft paper.

Border strips

A number of different types of cut corrugated borders are available. They can be painted to suit.

Plinths

Cut pieces of card as shown and fix with Selotape on the inside edges. Fix a solid card circle to form a flat surface for mounting light artefacts on.

Larger displays or play set

Corrugated card can be used for play sets or large displays. See the Viking display on page 18. Untidy areas can be quickly transformed. The card can be sculpted around classroom features (pipes and tables). Ends of the corrugated roll can be used as mini-columns or folded over and stapled to firm walls. Drawing forward 'walls' of card can produce a surprisingly large mounting surface. Before starting check:

- that the walls are solid enough to staple.
- that electrical points are not made inaccessible.
- you measure carefully how much card is needed.

3D features

Many display features can be made with corrugated card. See the Roman temple on page 72.

Fixing artwork

1 Use pins as shown.
2 Use double-sided Selotape.
3 Use a light touch of Copydex in corners.

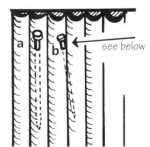

see below

Use pins as above in a) push vertically down the corrugation, not across as in b).

Lettering

Essentials

Do it right

Lettering must be clear and the style appropriate to the type and theme of a display. Remember that labelling should have a number of functions: it can question, decorate, acquaint, tell, clue, warn, advise, suggest or prompt, instruct or direct and inform. Generally speaking, speed is an important factor for the busy teacher. Here are a few ideas.

Titles

Titles need to be bold and large. They can be produced by tracing round templates, from pop out lettering, hand drafting or computers.

Spacing

Whether you use pop out lettering, templates, or hand drafting, it is essential that you get the spacing right. Upright letters can be spaced evenly whereas A, V, W and Y should be brought closer together, especially in words like WAVE.

Pop out letters

Simple to use, ready cut letters are available in 50 mm and 100 mm sizes and in seven colours. They can be used in a number of ways so that the cost can be kept quite low. Letters can be stippled or sprayed with variegated paints to colour match with the display. Once the letters have been used, the backing sheet can be used as a stencil and the letters themselves can be used as templates.

Hand drafting

1 Use light pencil lines as rough guides for top, centre and baselines for titles as shown below.

2 Make a centre line and work outwards.

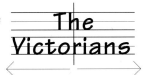
The
Victorians

3 Sketch letters in pencil.

4 Go over pencil outlines with thick felt tip pens.

Other lettering ideas

Commercial lettering

Contact local sign and display shops to borrow a range of different types of lettering to use as a feature in displays on writing or communications. See 1 and 2 below.

Three D effects

Use white or coloured craft paper to make sculptured letters. See 3 and 4 below. These can be used as large first letters of words or for the whole title. For all letters, you need to draw sets of parallel lines on the reverse of the letter. For example, an S can be drawn with three or five parallel lines (two lines form the outline). Score along the internal lines and crease them to give a really 3D effect as in the photo and the illustration bottom left. Other 3D effects can be achieved as follows:

- Mount cut out letters away from the background (use toilet rolls as spacers).
- Mount letters as mobiles.

Wooden templates

For cut out letters, reverse template and trace around. This stops any unwanted marks being produced on the front of letters. For continuous titles, draw faint pencil baseline and trace around templates carefully using felt tip pens (POSCA felt tips are good for this). See 5 below left.

Pop out and cut out lettering

Pop out lettering can be coloured by stippling, pad printing or marbling or can be colour washed.

Computer lettering

Labelling for displays can be done by using the school's computer and printer. Typefaces such as *Sassoon Primary* (see below) should be used if possible as they are very legible and reinforce good handwriting practice. Overuse of computer lettering is boring. Try adding borders or revert to simple clear hand lettering such as the Roman below.

Roman lettering

Simple Roman lettering combines lines that are straight, circular or nearly circular. Letters have got different widths. Some, M and A, fit exactly to a square, some are narrower. Only W is wider.

1 and 2 commercial
   display lettering.
3 Paper sculpture lettering.
4 Three D effect lettering.

5 Wooden template.
6 Pop out and cut out
   lettering.
7 Computer lettering.

LMNOP QRSTU VWXYZ

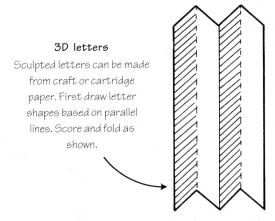

3D letters
Sculpted letters can be made from craft or cartridge paper. First draw letter shapes based on parallel lines. Score and fold as shown.

This is an example of Sassoon typeface.

Backings & borders

Planning displays

Gathering materials

With pressures on time it is all the more important to plan and gather resources efficiently, so that all the elements can be integrated within an overall colour scheme. Backings, borders and edging strips for tables are the vital first stages in a visually interesting display.

Matching and contrasting elements

Topics such as the seasons, celebrations and colour lend themselves to strong use of colour as a coordinating feature. Try out colours on scrap paper before sponge printing large areas of expensive poster papers. A plain fabric background often can give a display a stylish look (see page 54). On occasions complementary pairs of colours, blue and orange, red and green, purple and yellow, can also produce dazzling results, especially when close tints and tones of the base colours are used. A patchwork quilt can also be used (see below).

Chequer board pattern

Use coordinated colours and tones of poster papers to add interest to display backings (on page 12 the backing is a combination of two tones of green placed diagonally). As a variation on this two tone backing, you can add more colours or a third tone of the base colour, as in page 23 where a family of yellows and beiges are not simply laid edge to edge but are offset to produce a more interesting effect.

Border strips

Borders can be:
* Made by children (fold and cut paper figures).
* Ready made frieze, coloured and decorated.
* Ingersley poster borders. Ready made two inch rolls of poster paper (also in gold and silver).

Examples can be found throughout the book. Below is an example of a corrugated paper border.

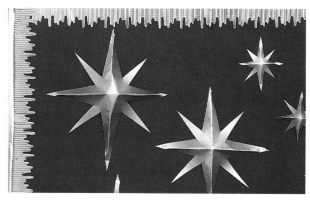

Hand printed backings

The photograph below shows a section of backing paper that has been printed by children. They used found objects: round, square, open and solid, to print over a large area of poster paper. The colours used are predominantly red and yellow which match the edging strips and the double mounts for the art works. This is an ideal and friendly backing for the infants' own lively pictures and writing accompanied by a flying teddy and other toys. Rolls of poster paper are good for this work as strips can be worked and rolled up as you go.

Mounting & fixing

Mounting

Step by step

Whether single, double or triple mounting is used, the first step is to trim the artwork or writing so that it is a regular shape. Single mounting is enhanced if fine lines are painted on the inside edge of the mount. Choose colours carefully in advance. Double and triple mounts make more of the work but the same simple procedure applies.

Ready cut mounts

NES Arnold produce excellent packs of matching sugar papers cut ready for multiple mounting. Also, Slater Harrison produce A4 plus poster mounts in a range of colours. Using these, simply take A4 sized artwork and mount in the centre of the backing paper. For extra accuracy, place artwork in position first and mark top two corners with pencil on the poster paper. Card window mounts can be covered with colour coordinated fabrics as shown below. (See photograph on page 38).

Self-adhesive mounts

For extra special occasions try the ready cut, self-adhesive card mounts in muted colours (Slater Harrison). Clik frames offer another alternative.

Fixing artwork

There are many ways of fixing artwork. Staple guns save time, but try to hide the staples. Selotape, double sided and magic tape are all useful. Selotape can be used to mask areas for fine painted edges. Blutack, PVA and Pritstick are methods of fixing things in place. To remove Blutack, use another small piece to pick up scraps from the wall or mount. Velcro is ideal for fixing to Expoloop. The photograph below shows an interesting way of displaying a sequence of pages using pins.

Resources

Self-adhesive card mounts, sugar paper, blue poster paper, poster mounts, found objects

1 Cut window mount.

2 Cut fabric to cover card mount.

3 Fix fabric over window mount.

3D effects

Use cut out shapes of different tones as mounts to give 3D effect.

Our World Display

The display

Display includes flag border, artefacts, books, stimulus questions and outline maps. Backing paper is pale green and leaf green checkerboard in Ingersley poster paper (710 X 760 mm sheets), border in leaf green and lemon yellow. Complete the border by Blu-tacking flag quarters randomly over yellow and green border strips. Flag cards available from Child's Play International. Include a range of artefacts and books.

1 Cut eight 15 cm diameter blue circles.

2 Cut green paper rounded letters.

Title lettering

3 String between two halves of world

Making 3D arrows

1 Make template.

2 Make up straight or curved arrows.

3 Score lightly along centre lines.

4 crease and fold.

5 Blu-tack to fix.

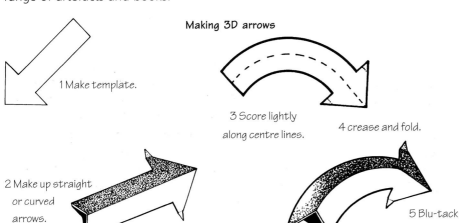

Resources

Maps, animal pictures books, artefacts, map cards, cards, paper, fabrics

Our world

Topic ideas

Discuss differences and similarities in life around the world. Talk about the effect of weather on places and life. How has the way we live and our environment changed over time? What threats are there to our environment? Talk about myths and legends of creation. Get your children to observe, record and communicate what they notice about places, local and faraway. What makes it possible to live where we do (warmth, air, food, and shelter)?

Make 'Our World' batik or appliqué wall hangings, volcano friezes (*Dinosaurs and all that rubbish*). Make paints from earth and charcoal. Look at paintings showing our world and use these to stimulate children's work (Hellenistic frescoes, Martini's and Giotto's frescoes, *The young St. John* by Giovanni Di Paolo, *The Journey of the Magi* by Benozzo Gozzoli, scenes from the *Très Riches Heures du Duc de Berry*, *The Fall of Icarus* by Pieter Breughel, Rousseau's jungle pictures and works by Constable, Turner, Claude Lorrain, Poussin and the Impressionists). Use multi-cultural artefacts.

Design different flags for countries. Make vehicles for crossing different terrains (swamp, desert, snow, mountains). Cook different foods from around the world. Make food like different features (rivers, mountains, volcanoes).

Write about favourite places (poems and prose). Read Narnia books, *The Enchanted Wood*, *Journey to the Centre of the Earth*, *Round the World in 80 days*. Write about school conservation area and wildlife.

Look at features of our world (hills, rivers, seas, volcanoes, islands) and at the school, local town, country and continents on different scale maps. Compass points. Discuss the use of land in different countries, the quality of life/different environments around the world. The importance of location for weather/climate/communications. Design layouts for the school ponds/conservation areas. Use symbols for different forms of plant/animals.

Discoverers and explorers such as Columbus. Time-lines of the universe, prehistory and history. Ancient and national costumes. Tools through the ages.

Measurement. Sets (animals). Comparing measurements, sizes and shapes (distances between planets, height of mountains, size of countries and populations).

Beethoven's *Pastoral*, *Stars* by Simply Red, *With a little help from my friends* by the Beatles, *Trains and boats and planes*, *Atomizer* by Andy Murray, *Lion King* soundtrack.

Read a range of creation stories, story of Noah.

Plant, animal and human life. Food chains. Materials, energy, position of the earth in space, the 'big bang theory'

Try these

Banana game (Oxfam)

Use the Oxfam survival farming activity pack which includes the banana game. It is truly cross-curricular and involves children in difficult planning and decision making processes. Work in groups of different sizes, such as three, four, five or six to emulate typical working family sizes. This activity can be extended from one morning to a day or take up a whole week.

World in a supermarket bag (Oxfam)

Work in groups. Unpack a supermarket bag. Identify countries of origin and the cost of each item. Tabulate and display information for the whole class. Create a class world map (paper on floor). Label with each country of origin and the products. Ask questions such as: Why are some foods expensive and others cheap? Use worksheets. Use the map for routes of trade and word recognition games.

Italian market stall

The display

Model and paint/glaze pizzas, bananas, pasta, plates of Italian food. Fix firmly on market stall. Fix four canes (wrapped and finished in red and black crepe paper with added bows) to a table. Use boxes to give height. Cover the table with sacking. Strips of red, white and green crepe make a canopy. Add lettering and labels: red, green and white letters on a pink card.

Topic ideas

Talk about markets (car boots to EU) and ways/ places of selling: kiosks, churches, schools, streets, bazaars, airports, via newspapers/TV. Make a trip to market and record different activities. Your class can make its own shop.

Resources

Dry foods, sweets, paint sprays, paper, pencils, newspaper, scrap materials

Look at the history of trading, fairs, early forms of bartering and money, tokens and various other ways of paying.

Model and paint foods. Make pictures with pasta and pulses. Spray pasta for Christmas cards/calendars. Look at pictures showing foods.

Design and make: stalls, food, money, posters advertising foods, packaging for fragile foods (eggs) or unusual shapes (bananas), seasonal carrier bags, clothes for market traders.

Create a menu for a restaurant and link with maths activity of planning restaurant dinner to cost £5.00. Write advertising slogans, packaging labels, menu poems. Read poems and stories about famous fairs and markets. Match places for buying and selling with different products.

Maps of food found in different places. Trade between countries, forms of transport for different products- strawberries, cars, bananas, milk, televisions.

Design a pizza using different toppings. Make the maximum number of varieties from a specific number of toppings. Infants' shopping activities leading to science and language activities. Use money, exchange pounds for other currencies, measure, estimate, scale and weigh materials.

Songs: *Scarborough fair, Ba-Ba Blacksheep, Tom-Tom the Piper's sons, Fish 'n' Chips* (round), *Cockles and Mussels*, the theme *to Banana Splits, Oranges and Lemons, Food* from *Oliver, Banana boat song, Sing a Song of sixpence, Little Miss Muffit.*

Talk about Jesus in the temple throwing out the merchants and morality of trading: is it right to buy and sell anywhere and any time? Discuss cheating, fairness, weighing and checking. Food for celebrations. Feeding of the five thousand.

Create a balanced diet. Investigate: changes in materials, melting cheese, boiling pasta, seasons for produce, quality of produce, fair testing, measuring solids and liquids. Talk about ways of food preservation throughout the ages, including freezing and food hygiene and safety. Make a survey of favourite foods.

Deep in the woods

The display

This nursery rhymes display combines oatmeal backing paper with wallpaper border, grasses, baskets, sections of wood, model cottages ,fabrics. The work is double mounted on gold and black.

Topic ideas
Read various versions of different fairy stories. Try *Ten in a bed* by Alan Ahlberg.

 Draw and paint cottages and story characters. Make puppets and miniature theatres (write plays for them). Use pictures to retell stories, sequence and rearrange for different endings. Make flicker book to show action within the story.

Make little cottages (from food or sweets), Piggy's house from scraps (test materials for strength), wolf with flashing eyes, a quilt for Goldilocks's bed, invitations to the Three Little Pigs' housewarming party or monster rave party. Design new front cover for rewritten story. Write a fairy menu.

Map Goldilocks' journey. Use papier maché to make imaginary woods with creatures and magical foods.

Count teddies in units, tens and hundreds, tessellate patterns for quilts.

Use reflective materials to make magic mirrors and test different materials to make houses.

 Write stories from jumbled tales, beginnings, endings, characters, places. Rewrite the ending of a story. Predict a story from its front cover. Write a book review. Older children write stories with high frequency words for infants.

Nursery rhymes, rhythmic sounds *Fee Fi Fo Fum* (sound effect stories), *Strawberry fields for ever*, *Country roads* by John Denver.

Good and evil, strange places, stranger danger.

Try these

Was Goldilocks guilty?
Divide class into groups (for and against on opposite sides of the classroom) and two speakers. As the children are persuaded by the arguments, they change sides. Write up the case as a newspaper story.

Guided fantasy
Relax children for a few minutes, then with eyes closed listen to a story—'I am walking, what do you see?' Talk about and write up their experience.

She is guilty!

The display

This is a record of a school trip. Free standing boards are edged with black. A whole range of artefacts, cardboard, beach hats are mounted directly onto light blue and white striped wallpaper. Seagull mobiles from painted plywood (see illustration on next page), starfish, shells, children's own works and visit records are arranged together.

Class books include *A fisherman's tale* (marbled with blue fabric edging and vertical lettering) and *Jonah and the whale.* This lovely display features an old tin, (full of shells and crabs), that has been stencilled along its edges in blue. Children's artworks are rolled and folded away from the board for 3D effect (see illustration on following page).

Seaside

Topic ideas

Discuss before making the trip, what to see and collect. Talk about habitats and ecosystems, identifying live and dead creatures. Make little sketch books/journals to use on the trip.

Collect, sort and make paintings of pebbles, shells, flotsam and jetsam. Paint designs on pebbles, varnish them. Sketch seagulls, pears, Punch and Judy, donkeys and fish and chip shops. Photograph seaside subjects: signs, souvenirs, amusements.

Design and make: seaside peepshow (small hall of mirrors), a brochure to promote the seaside resort, souvenirs, scary rides and bathing huts.

Retell tales of trips, (favourite/most awful), how and where I went on my last holidays. Make class books: A history of seaside towns.

Map holidays on world map. Use seaside town as part of coastal environment project.

Victorian spas and seaside towns. Look at early railway posters

Time tables, speed calculations (distance and time), fairs, sorting pebbles according to weight and size. Count species in pools, make graphs of results.

Shanties, Carousel, Surfer girl (Beach Boys), Sitting on the dock of the bay (Otis Redding), Watermark CD (Enya)- including On your shore and Sail away.

Jonah and the whale, the baptism of Christ, Moses and the parting of the sea, the feeding of the five thousand.

Investigate the different habitats and ecosystems. Classify items according to living, non-living and dead. Study rock pool life and food chains. Make and use telescopes. Consider the health of sailors in days gone by, the need for fruit and vegetables and the importance of a balanced diet.

1 Mount on backing paper.

Displaying work

The sun and the sea

3 Curve paper and pin agin.

2 Pin top corners in place.

Side

End

Roof

1 Cut six pieces of card.

Bathing hut

2 Cut door to form hinge.

3 Fix and glue tabs, paint and mount.

Seagull mobile

1 Make designs from sketches made on trip.

2 Trace body and wing shapes onto balsa or plywood.

3 Cut, assemble and paint.

Vikings

The display

It features the use of corrugated card, and children's soft toys as models for Viking soldiers. See page 7 for other uses of corrugated card.

Topic ideas

Carve ornate figure heads for Viking ship, use snake and dragon motifs. Paint pictures based on myths.

Model armour and costumes on soft toys. Design Viking ships and weapons (string glued on card under foil for embossed finish).

Read story of Thor's stolen hammer. Write own epic tales and the diary of a Viking.

Make time lines of children back to the time of the Vikings. Read about famous explorers and write about journeys into the unknown.

Investigate sinking and floating. Make a stone float. Use various materials for sails.

Which shapes are best for sails? Measure and estimate.

Resources

Corrugated card, glue, string, soft toys, foil, chocolate coins, card, jewellery, wood, books, craft paper, face paints

Try this

Cut a strip of corrugated card. Score, fold and glue to make a shelf unit as in the photo. Fit corrugated surfaces of display backing and shelf together.

Land ahoy!

The display

Red background with black border. Treasure chest made from painted cut out card with jewellery and coins (chocolate ones) hanging out. Add pieces of wood painted with images of ships or pirates or made up to look like ship wrecks. Paint square wooden tiles with strong colourful images and scatter throughout the display. Include illustrated books on pirates and buccaneers. Display them so that the pages can be turned and the story read.

Topic ideas

From cut craft paper make parrots, coconuts and other desert island pictures. Make pirate masks and use face paints for tattoos. Discuss the flood of Noah's ark. Paint pictures of before and after the flood.

Imaginative writing. Re-present stories such as *Treasure Island, Robinson Crusoe, The Moonstone, Grandpa* (John Burningham).

Mapping, finding treasure. Name places and features around the world. Discuss sources of water, seas and rivers.

Try this

Crossing the sea

Give children the following characters: a wolf, a goat, a cabbage and a sailor. The sailor has to make sure that he gets everything from the port to the island in the shortest number of moves possible. The boat is too small to take all three at once. His problem is that the wolf and goat can't be left together, nor the goat and the cabbage. How does the sailor solve the problem?

Examine artefacts from previous ages, finding evidence and interpreting it. Make treasure for future discoverers. Consider what is precious today. What represents our culture? Do an archeology game; one group makes ancient artefacts and hides them whilst the others find and try to interpret them.

What things are needed for a voyage? How much space is there to store the supplies? Work out the volumes. Make a list, set priorities and modify the list according to the space available.

When I was a baby

The display

In the display there are nursery colours, striped wallpaper in blue, yellow and white and wallpaper border, with the title cut out from blue frieze paper. Make the string netting as shown below.

Topic ideas

Each child makes a *Diary of my life*. Make a family tree and timeline, and link with history topics such as Victorians or Egyptians.

Who is who? Make a photo gallery of selves and relatives as babies. Is there a family resemblance? Paint self-portraits as part of a Welcome class picture. Add names and favourite toys, friends, foods or activities.

Talk about problems of growing up. Relate this with the metamorphosis of butterflies, tadpoles and the idea of change and ageing. Sex education for older children.

Investigate the five senses. Do simple cooking involving health, food and hygiene. How does food help us grow? Make a list of the things that children can do with their bodies (for example, dancing, swimming, listening) and things they are good at. Can babies do all of these things? Discuss caring for babies and testing bath water with elbows to check the temperature. Play with dolls, washing and drying them.

Make comparisons and find differences between babies, children and adults. Find out how tall and heavy the children were as babies; how tall and heavy are they now? Make simple graphs of their height, weight and sizes of hands and length of stride.

Simple reportive writing about themselves as babies and brothers and sisters. Imaginative writing about their feelings and best memories.

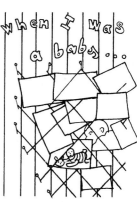

Netting for displays

Resources

Blue wallpaper, paints, borders, frieze paper, photographs, scraps, cardboard cartons, tissue paper, foil, models of eyes, balloons

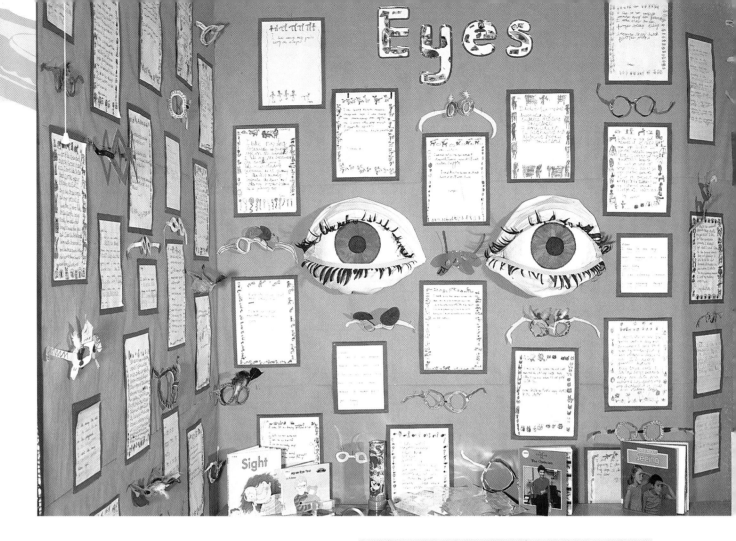

Eyes display

Paste layers of tissue paper over inflated balloon, when dry cut in half lengthwise, build up with papier maché and paint white to make up 3D eyes. Cut circles of paper for the pupils, paint and stick in place. Use strips of pink paper for the eyelids and cut strips of black paper for the eyelashes.

Topic ideas

Make designer glasses using scraps in an imaginative way. Look through things such as toilet rolls to make round pictures. Make textured pictures for blind people. Make galleries of *Amazing things we've seen* and touch pictures.

Talk about seeing things and the way eyes work. Borrow models of eyes. Draw and name the different parts of the eyes and write about their functions. Why are some people colour blind? Make colour studies of houses or landscapes and invert the colours (use red for trees, blue for roofs and yellow for skies). See how light is bent in the school pond (rushes and reeds appear bent). Use prisms, refraction grids, kaleidoscopes.

Try this

Walk in camera obscura

Cut door in a child sized cardboard carton as shown below. Make 2 by 2 cm hole in one side of carton. Make a small hole in a piece of thick foil, place over the hole in the carton. Opposite the aperture paste white paper. Place the camera near bright window for good view. Children take turns and paint upside down pictures.

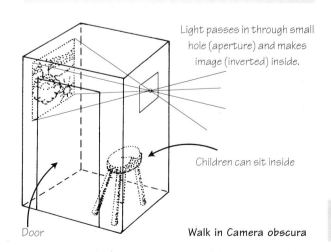

Light passes in through small hole (aperture) and makes image (inverted) inside.

Children can sit inside

Door

Walk in Camera obscura

We've arrived

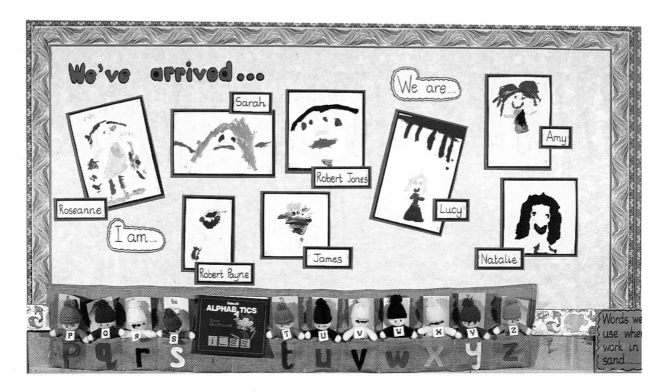

The display

A simple but important display celebrating the arrival of children in school. Their names and first self-portraits are double mounted on black and red paper, while the title is in the same two colours. In the front are soft toys asleep in their alphabet sleeping bags. The pretty border to the soft backing paper reinforces a homely feel to the classroom.

Topic ideas

Roll out small slabs of clay and press hands or feet into them, making an impression. Write the names underneath, dry, fire and glaze. Cut from a thin slab of clay a face outline, roll balls for noses and eyes, sausage shapes for mouths and hair. Fix the parts together using slip (liquid clay). Dry, fire and colour.

Design and make happy/sad paper plate puppets. Named self-portraits on two plates can be stuck together and hung to form a mobile or used as puppets for role play. This activity can be extended by making clothes from crepe paper or scrap fabrics. The clothes can be designed to keep the children warm on their way to school.

Make a simple *This is me* book to include children's favourite activities, friends, holidays and food. Ask children to describe themselves and have a helper to write it down. Children can then draw and use simple IT programmes. Talk about the children's names and about the origins and meanings of names and surnames.

This display links with arrivals of all kinds. Arrange a trip to a farm or nature reserve. Look for chicks and various baby animals. Make a scrap book and include pictures of animals, their life cycles and aspects of the environment such as wild flowers.

Portraits

The display

Print or stencil the border with colours that match the backing papers and artwork. Mount pictures and written work on black card, trim to produce an even and relatively thin edging. Use three or four shades of similar colours of backing paper and arrange them as shown, overlapping slightly to make an interesting effect. Arrange title and pictures carefully before fixing. Then position pen portraits in place overlapping slightly into the pictures.

Topic ideas

 Experiment with line work using pencil charcoal and pastel. Draw backs of heads, make quick sketches of classmates without heads and arrange a *Guess who* gallery. Use sugar paper to make huge torn drawings of friends. Make a silhouette gallery. Do self-portraits as animals or as objects with faces. Make identikit portraits, made from individual drawings of eyes, noses, ears fixed together on a basic face shape. Make texture portraits, collage, appliqué using soft and hard materials. Make clay portraits either solid or from a slab of clay cut to face outline.

Make pen portraits of how things felt when *I was angry, ill* or *happy*.

What can you tell about people from looking at portraits? Tudors, the Stuarts and the Victorians, all looked different. Look at famous group portraits. Who is rich, who is poor? What is happening in the picture? Do role play based on it.

Investigate the jobs that the nose, ears, eyes, fingers and tongue do. Make taste and listening galleries. Collect photographs to show how faces change as you grow older.

Ask questions such as: Are your eyes near the top or the bottom of your head? How wide are your mouths? Then measure faces of all the class. Make charts of the height and width of heads. Measure the relative position of features on faces. Can you produce an average face? Are faces symmetrical? What does a symmetrical face look like? Draw and model some.

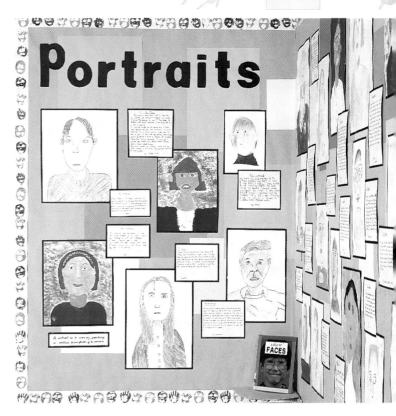

Headless portraits

Resources

Cream border strip, clay, potatoes (for printing), paints, pencils, black card, fabrics, Modroc, charcoal, sugar paper, glue

23

How my body works

The display

Mount cut out bones on black edging for border. Print bones from card plates onto fabric (making interesting falling pattern of bones). Collect written work, pictures, and make hanging labels with questions on one side. Make sectional views of the body, with cut out and raised ribs and intestines all labelled. Cover tables with cotton and drape bone fabric.

Topic ideas

Make head from papier maché, remove parts to reveal the eyes. Make feet mobiles: draw round feet, cut out, paint, name and hang. Make a 'hand tree': paint a trunk on a large piece of paper, children paint their hands and then press in position up the trunk to form the tree. Mix paints to match hand colours: paint picture of hands (paint patches on hands to check colours). Use hand prints to make happy and sad faces. Press hands in clay. Look at hands by Durer, Giacommetti and Cassat.

Make illuminated class book. Make feet and hand poems. Give each child a piece of paper that is divided into boxes (one per pupil), with their name on it. Everyone writes a nice comment.

Early humans, changes over time, family tree, history of school and community.

Data handling, height, weight, ways of presenting class information from the questionnaire. Body maths using non-standard measurements to give a description of the classroom (see *Try these* on next page).

Arrange class as a body system (some dressed in red as the blood). Use music to provide the beat of the heart as the blood moves around.

Undertake a fitness testing over a period of six weeks, see changes, gather data and present it. What happens during and after exercising? Make up lungs from plastic bags. As part of study of the digestive system, write a diary of a baked bean. As children find out the answers to the questions posed in the display, write the answers on the reverse of the mobile labels. These will rotate and remind the children in a fun way. Investigate how senses work. How is sound received? Look at models of ears and classify sounds. Invent sign language.

Stories from the Bible, write poetry about hands that care, share, embrace and welcome.

24

Funny bones

The display

Borders of white hands on 15 cm wide black strip.
Make mobiles from children's skeleton cut outs.
Add books to do with funny bones and children's
own books made with concertina designs.

Topic ideas

 Make skeletons with art straws on black paper. Make skeleton costumes for drama.

 Make hinged joints as shown below and use pulleys and levers as mechanical joints.

 Higher order reading skills. Ahlberg's *Funny Bones* book.

 Make display of replica skulls to go with rocks and fossils.

 Egyptian mummies, burial mounds.

 Draw, label and identify bones. Draw and cut hinged joints from wood. How do they work? Make a bones and fossils gallery.

Discuss Jesus' death and resurrection. Find similar events in other religions including Buddhism and talk about the idea of eternal life.

Try these

Hand shakes: Make groups of four and ask "if each of you shakes hands with every other group member, how many times will you shake hands?" Once they work this out, work in bigger groups and try to estimate and work out a formula.

Untangle: Group children in ten or more. Link their hands in a chaotic way. Ask them to untangle themselves so that they make a circle. They have to work as a group to solve the problem.

Resources

Rubber bands, strong card, labels, paper fasteners, old sheet, black border paper, backing papers, black fabric dye, models

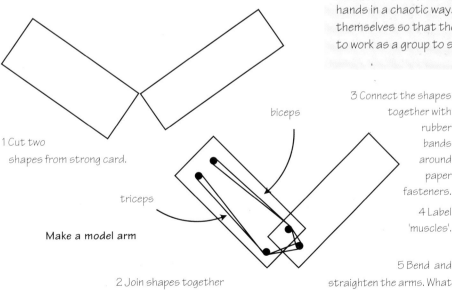

1 Cut two shapes from strong card.

Make a model arm

2 Join shapes together with paper fastener.

biceps

triceps

3 Connect the shapes together with rubber bands around paper fasteners.

4 Label 'muscles'.

5 Bend and straighten the arms. What happens to the 'muscles'?

Homes

The display

The display board is covered with white and light blue motif fabric, surrounded by blue poster paper border. The title is from white cut out letters edged with a blue felt tip pen and strung between a block of flats, house and a tree (animal homes). Talk about homes for humans, toys, animals and plants. Include a variety of resources to stimulate comparison and discussion: mice living in flower pots, books, childrens' toys, historical and contemporary multi-cultural domestic artefacts, photographs and posters. Use questions in the display such as: can you make a home for your toys? Where do you live? What is an African home like? What was it like living in a cave?

Resources

Clay, nylon, cotton, photographs, glazes, felt tip pens, moss, wood, sketch books, coloured pencils, wax crayons, artefacts

26

Topic ideas

In sketch books, make coloured drawings of children's homes and gardens. Use these to make a class frieze of a whole street including each house (try batik on paper for special effects). With clay make small tiles, press, mark and model the surface with a picture of a home. Glaze with colours. Make rubbings from different building materials, try red, black and yellow papers as a change from white. Make clay models of derelict houses. Make a trip to town, draw homes, then find and name the main parts of the buildings.

Use squared paper and card to plan, scale and redesign bedrooms. Then make models from cardboard boxes and finish with furniture and fabrics made from scraps. Design and make life-sized shelters. Use strong structures. Rain and wind test in the school grounds. Try natural and made materials like nylon, cotton, leaves, moss and wood. Design the right house for the little pigs.

Use cardboard boxes and newspaper to make a cave dwelling in the home corner of the classroom. Decorate the inside with cave paintings. What was a Roman kitchen like? Make a model of a Roman house. Study castles and the development of distinct styles of architecture. Study the development of domestic pottery and tools, for example see how light bulbs are recycled in Africa as kerosene lamps.

Abraham and his tent. Noah's ark, places of worship, Jesus in the stable, world problems of homeless people.

Write about the functions of homes: physical security, education, relaxation and the benefits of a loving, calm and attractive environment. Write about 'My ideal home' (size, shape, materials). Imagine three impossible, wonderful things to have inside the ideal house. Compare the ideal house with a real one on one piece of paper; include writing and pictures.

Strong and weak shapes, angles. Make a survey of children's homes, present data in graphs.

Investigate to find strong structures and materials for building purposes.

Try this

Home in space: Cut four hexagons and three squares (60 cm sides) from sheets of thick cardboard. Cut diagonally two of the squares in half. Make large geodesic dome as shown below. Make a door and fit the space home with controls, radios and all the equipment needed for survival. Will the space people land on a strange planet?

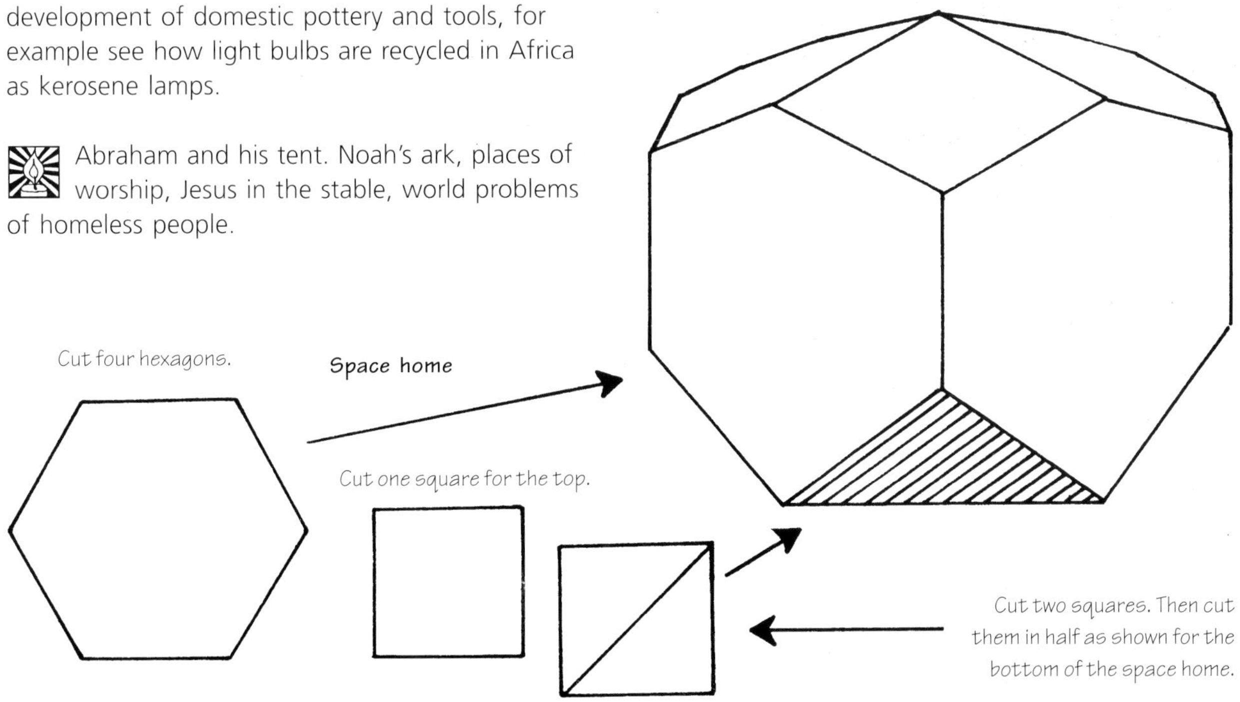

Cut four hexagons.

Space home

Cut one square for the top.

Cut two squares. Then cut them in half as shown for the bottom of the space home.

Victorian homes

Cosy corner

Make believe

In every classroom, an area can be used to create make believe worlds. The photograph shows an old fire place fixed to a wall which has been papered with Victorian style paper. The front parlour is completed with a washing line, drying some old clothes, whilst the mantel piece is home to teddy bears, rocking horses, little cups and saucers, pressed flowers and old photographs. In front is an old wooden chair and table that is not just decorative but an area where children sit and work as if they were Victorian school children.

Other home ideas

- Space stations.
- Cave homes.
- Planet 'X'.
- Iron age hut.
- Atlantis.
- Ship wreck.

Try this

Upstairs downstairs: Show pictures of Victorian homes and discuss the different jobs people did in those days. Some people were maids, squires, nannies whilst others worked in factories, in the fields or were vicars, nurses or soldiers. Choose a Victorian story such as *The Christmas Carol* and use some of the characters for your own simplified Victorian sketch. Make a hat for each character that you choose. Role play the scenes with each child wearing a hat and acting the character. Change the hats during the role play so that children live through something of what it was like to be in positions of authority, servitude, respect, wealth and poverty.

Resources

Photographs, wood, artefacts, clothes, old fire place, card, washing line, teddy bears, chair, table, cups and saucers, dry flowers

Victorian nursery

The display

Children's written work mounted on a light background is accompanied by small three dimensional pieces supported on the backing board.

Topic ideas

Collect photographs and artefacts from olden days and mount an old and new display. Discuss the social conditions and how children used to work like slaves. Compare with the world today. Compare children's timetables in schools. Have a Victorian day in school dressed up with period clothing (work as near as possible to a full day). Make a class book of generations including cut out photographs of people of different ages. Include written work on aspects of life that have changed.

Stencil Victorian tile patterns. Make miniature silhouettes and costume dolls.

Discuss changes in communications, road, rail, telegraph, canals. Wire up simple Morse key with batteries from one class to another. How has farming changed since Victorian days?

Make Victorian artefacts using the authentic materials; make small wooden rocking horses as shown below. Make and cook gingerbread men. Look at the engineering work of Brunel who designed ships and bridges. Design nursery frieze.

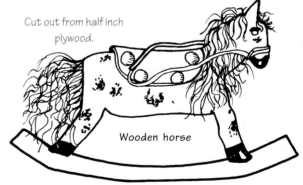

Cut out from half inch plywood.

Wooden horse

Re-present nursery rhymes, write some for future generations. Make a list of things that Victorians did and did not have such as TV, plastics and computers.

Investigate changes to water as it is heated and cooled. The Victorian age of steam power accelerated the Industrial Revolution.

Favourite toys display

Collect dolls, soft toys, construction toys, toys with wheels and some cardboard boxes. Print over blue backing paper with a bright interesting pattern. Use a simple red border with a title made from similar poster paper. Double mount the artwork using red and black poster papers or thin card. Mount written work with a thin black border. Make captions and questions using white, red or blue card. Fix artwork and toys to the backing paper and arrange other toys in front.

Try this

Naughty toys

Children bring in to school a soft toy. The toys will stay in school overnight. When the children go home take the toys and put them in unusual places around the classroom such as tops of cupboards or hanging from the ceiling. In the morning ask how did the toys get there? Did they have a party? How can they get down? The children design and make vehicles to retrieve their toys.

Topic ideas

 Make a gallery of pictures of favourite toys.

Make toys' houses from boxes and scrap materials. Design toys with moving parts. Design and make a stuffed toy (transfer design to felt by tracing with white chalk). Design a toy as a means of transport. Design a toy for an adult to enjoy. Make a toy that creates a musical sound.

Write about favourite toys: Why are they favourites? Tell stories about the toys' adventures.

Make a survey. Which toys do most children like? How many like dolls the best? Present data in attractive graphs.

Investigate forces. How fast will cars go down slopes? Make a Lego car that can move a certain distance.

Make musical toys.

The toy shop window

The display

Shop window style displays can be most effective as they are inviting. For this toy shop, use finely striped backing paper with a bold black border to give an impression of looking into a window. Double mount children's work with matching coloured paper and fine black edging. Mount some so that corners of written work can be lifted to read more work underneath, curl mount some work to give variety. Arrange children's work with a collection of painted soldiers, small figures, masks and postcards and then fix in place with dress makers' pins. To enhance the shop window impression:

- Add thin black paper window bars across the display.
- Cut and fix price tickets and stick in place behind the window bars.
- Make an open/closed label and fix behind a make believe door.
- Mount behind windows along corridor.

My toy comes alive

Another way of adding interest is to include 3D features to displays. The photograph below shows a lively figure from a display on *My toy comes alive*.

Resources

Striped backing paper, toy soldiers, masks, postcards, scraps, pins, felt, chalks, dolls, soft toys, cardboard boxes

Bear displays

Dear Bear display

Cross-curricular toys

Children's toys can be used to introduce ideas in many subject areas. Here are a few suggestions.

How tall is your bear display

Ask the children to bring in lots of bears of different sizes. The border is made in a similar way to the Dear Bear display above. The central strip is white paper that has been marbled with two or three tones of yellow. This strip is mounted on a light yellow border that coordinates with the marbling. The main backing paper is black, whilst the title is cut out from yellow paper. Coloured cubes, pictures of some of the bears and information about the height of the bears complete the display board. The bears are simply arranged in front.

Topic ideas

Measure all the bears using multi-link cubes. Record the results and present them as shown or make a simple graph. Measure around the bears' heads with a fabric measure.

Use the measurements from above to make clothes to protect the bears from cold, rain or the sun. Use tissue paper to make up simple patterns for the clothes. Make a hat.

The display

The display board is covered with bright green poster paper. The border is made as shown. It is edged with a black border strip, onto this is mounted a white border roll that has been sponge printed with black and green blocks of colour. Artwork is triple mounted in green and black.

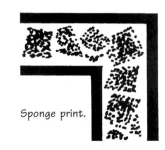

Sponge print.

Topic ideas

Imaginative writing and art are started off by a letter to the children (top of photo), from the bear in Mrs. Edgecumbe's cupboard. The children read and discussed the letter and then painted watercolour pictures of what they imagined the bear looked like and wrote letters to the *Bear in the Cupboard*

More display ideas

The history of the teddy bear

Teddy Bear can feature either as part of a general display on the history of toys or make a small wall display as shown below. Most children do not realise that teddy bears only date back to the beginning of the 20th century.

More topic ideas

Make a drawing of a country scene (show some of Rousseau's jungle scenes). Add teddy bears to the scene and paint.

Ask the children to redesign their home or bedroom so that it would be suitable for the three bears to live in.

Ask the children to imagine that they are either the mummy, daddy or baby bear. Write an account of Goldilocks' visit to their house. (see page 15 for the trial of Goldilocks).

More border ideas

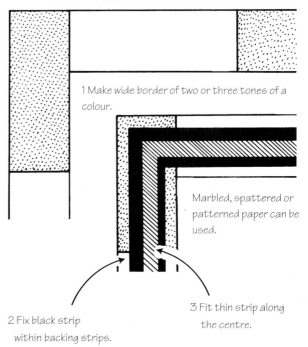

1 Make wide border of two or three tones of a colour.

Marbled, spattered or patterned paper can be used.

2 Fix black strip within backing strips.

3 Fit thin strip along the centre.

Goodnight Owl!

The display

Use light blue poster paper with dark blue border. The tree trunk and branches can be made from black, brown and green papers (or dark brown fabric). The leaves are from tissue paper and paint. The children can make little characters including buzzy bees, a squirrel, woodpecker, robin, doves, crows, starlings and sparrows. Some of them could be 2D and some 3D mobiles. Fix the trunk of the tree to the display boards as shown, bringing out the main branches to fill the upper branch. Fix the leaf shapes, and make the owl with bright yellow eyes, a 3D beak and wings as shown. The owl is painted in a range of tawny colours. Mount all birds and creatures to make the whole scene looking extremely busy.

Topic ideas

These ideas can be used with other books such as: *The owl who was afraid of the dark* and *Fergus' upside down day.*

Make wire sculpture of owl as below, printing and colour mixing (feathers, bark).

Investigate the order that the animals go down from the tree. Make graph of visitors to bird table. Make leaf and 3D shapes for beaks.

Read stories, start off imaginative writing about waking up in the dark, poetry about candles, reversing lettering (white on black for night time). Record visitors to bird table.

Empathy with living creatures, creation, night/dark, light/day. Right and wrong: if the children were the owl, what would they choose to do?

Design: a way of getting the owl to the ground, of switching off lights from distance, a bird table and nest building store as below.

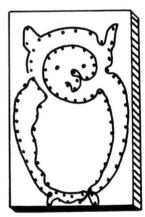

Creepy crawlies

1 Make clay body.

Make a bungy spider

2 Cut elastic bands in half for legs.

Web

Flies

Buzz

Spider

Web Pictures

Bugs

Legs

Spiders

The display

Discuss how spiders catch their food. Talk about webs, nets and all kinds of woven structures. Collect different types of baskets and nets to catch fish, to keep birds off fruit and even string vests to keep cold air out. Talk about the way spiders move. Play games such as crab football (children lie on their backs to start with and then arch themselves off the ground and run around like crabs).

Topic ideas

Use higher order reading skills with *Charlotte's web*. Write a diary of a spider (how it makes the web). Write a poem about catching flies. Label the different parts of insects and spiders. Role play using web, as in D&T below.

Classification: what makes an insect? Use your conservation area to investigate mini systems. Measure and enclose one square metre of land in two or three locations. Record the findings and compare them.

Create a large web in the corner of the room. Make bird's nest with authentic materials.

Construct child sized insects from boxes and scrap. Make close up paintings of small scenes of grass and insects in the mini system. Make web sculptures (small branch of tree woven with wool, shiny materials and string). Use thick cord stuck to card as a basis of an embossed web as shown (carefully rub down aluminium foil over the cord). Make bungy spiders on elastic bands as shown above. Use rough string and wool scraps to make open weaving on card looms.

Make charts with illustrations of the different insects found. Find out about the biggest and smallest spiders. Make diagrams to scale.

Resources

Poster, coloured and tissue papers, paints, baskets, books, nets, string, card, scraps

35

Birds and beasts

Peacock and hands displays

All kinds of animals can be made using hand prints. The peacock's body is made by curving out card from the display board and covering it with shiny blue materials. The hands are printed in yellow, blue, red, orange, violet and green. The radiated pattern off them is finished with golden circles fixed to the black background. Feely bags and questions about how different materials feel are included.

Topic ideas

Use hand prints to make pictures of hedgehogs and trees. Make up a helping hand display with writing about the way children help their parents/teacher and things that they can make. Use stencil designs of different birds for fabric decorations or class books on birds. Children can make growth patterns rather like the pattern on peacocks' tails. Start with a pastel dot and radiate from that all kinds of bands of colours in regular or irregular contours.

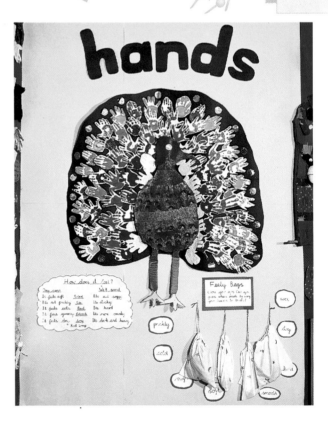

Enormous crocodile display

Great for a long corridor as a crocodile can wind its way along walls, around heaters, while it chases self-portraits of children! Make the body and tail from circles of different sizes, printed with lines of many colours. Printing the circles is done by folding them and dragging paint laden string from the centre out, making patterns. The head of the crocodile is made from half circles, whilst the nose and other features from quarter circles. The foliage is cut from two or three tones of green paper while the lettering is cut out from printed paper with a shadow effect as shown.

Topic ideas

 Use different shapes for different parts of the crocodile.

Plan and position the crocodile. Design and make a life-sized animal (or monster) with one moving part.

Imagine that friends have turned into monsters. Write about it. Make up names for monsters, some friendly and some fierce.

Try these

Cork crocodile: Use five or six corks of different sizes. Keep the largest cork for the head and cut a slit for the mouth. String the others together using wire. Cut groove in smallest cork to take the tail. Finish as shown.

Monster potato: Choose pointed potato. Scoop out the top, leaving a shell about 1 cm thick. Fix sequins for eyes, make tail from scrap materials. Put soil into the potato and sprinkle with cress seeds. Water regularly. Watch the monster grow.

Alive and growing

The display

The title is cut from green fabric and the background of grey fabric is surrounded by a carefully chosen wallpaper border. Between the mounted artwork, foliage is placed. Dressmakers' pins are used to secure the mounted work which can be heavy. A feature of the display is the way that the mounting of the work has been done with fabric covered card windows (see page 11).

Topic ideas

Make collages showing chicks in nests breaking from shells, pots of violets and pictures of trees.

Write acrostics, haiku and tanka poems about wild life, conservation, sunny and rainy days. Write accurate accounts about observations.

Design and make a simple incubator for hatching eggs.

Try this

Frequency and height of plants: Spread a line transect across part of the conservation area. Make stations 10 cm apart. Mark each one. Identify and count every specimen found at the station. Measure it and write it down on data collection forms. Make graphs with the results. Do other transects across the conservation area. Are the results the same?

Use the conservation area to find the average length of specific leaves. Measure ten leaves, number them and record the results. Make a line graph and work out the average length.

Collect and identify different species from pond dipping. Measure, name them and use magnifying glasses to draw diagrams ten times life size. Identify flowers and plants. Work in pairs, find flower or plant, draw it and then use the drawing with reference books for identification.

Jack & the Beanstalk

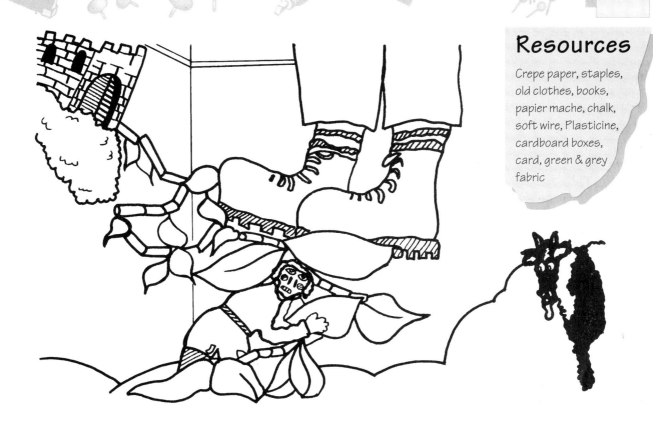

Resources

Crepe paper, staples, old clothes, books, papier mache, chalk, soft wire, Plasticine, cardboard boxes, card, green & grey fabric

The display

The beanstalk winds its way up a corner in the entrance hall. The giant, Jack and his mother are made from crepe paper stuck in place on stuffed old cloths. The figures are fixed firmly using heavy duty staples. A quiet reading area is arranged at the base of the beanstalk where children can read about giants, small creatures...

Topic ideas

Read nursery rhymes, *Gulliver's Travels, Alice in Wonderland, George's Marvellous Medicine* by Roal Dahl and other books to do with imaginary places and changes of scale. Do writing activities using *Story builders* such as characters, places and events. Start discussions with *Just supposing...*

Use the floor of the hall to draw with chalk the outline of a giant ten times bigger than an average child. Use pen, paper and calculators to work out the length and the breadth of the giant. Find out about the biggest and smallest human beings ever. Use black and white papers to make life-sized silhouettes of them.

With papier maché over soft wire frame make super large eating bowls and cutlery for the giant (make miniature versions with Plasticine). Make giants' heads using cardboard boxes (cut to fit over children's shoulders), finished with newspaper pasted to form a round shape. Paint and use in drama sessions.

Bake magic cakes or biscuits to change people's size (huge or small).

One, two, three!

The display

The display contains lots of ways of understanding numbers. Number cards, with one, two or three beads attached, flash cards with one frog, two soldiers and three bears are backed with a number patterned fabric that draws eyes down to a variety of number resources. Basket is home to class number toys and in the front are counting bricks, books and an abacus.

Topic ideas

Brainstorm what the world would be like without numbers and why numbers are important. Write counting poems: *One red carrot...*

History of numbers and calculation. Find out about rope folding method for parts of the whole. Explore non standard measures and the changing ways numbers have been written (Roman, Arabic, Chinese), tally counting, abacus and early calculators and computers.

Try these

Back numbers: Pin numbers on children's backs. The task is to find out what their own number is. They go around asking other children *Is it odd/ even, bigger or smaller than, divisible by, or palindromic?* Answers can only be Yes or No. This activity is differentiated by the difficulty of the number given. Try the game with shapes as well.

The calculator war: Split the class into three equal number groups: the brains, the calculators and the recorders. Make a table for scores on the blackboard. Call out a set number of problems such as: 5X5X5 or 2X10+3-7. The group of calculators have to wait until the answer appears before putting their hands up, the recorders have to write the calculation down completely, whereas the brains put their hand up as soon as they have worked out the answer. Score each correct answer for the teams until all the questions have been asked and the war is over.

Make palindromic numbers: Choose a three digit number, reverse it and add the two numbers together. If the result is not palindromic, reverse the digits in the results again and add these together. Make number chains. Play tables cowboys: two children stand as if in *High Noon* ready to shoot it out. The teacher calls out a multiplication from any table. The first child to call out the right answer and say *bang* is the winner. If the answer is not right, then the opponent has five seconds to get it right. If she doesn't, they both miss and go again.

Averages

How big display

Giant's footprints lead up from the display board across the ceiling to his castle on the other side of the classroom. The display board is covered with red poster paper. Around is a border of dark blue covered in feather images. Fabric printed with geometric shapes is draped behind a mini display of small units, balls, toys, sticks and calculators. Four fabric snakes and four Multilink men are accompanied by labels: *Short, long, longer, longest* and *short, tall, taller, tallest*.

Topic ideas

Measure how tall the children are, or how tall their bears are (see page 32). Line the children up from tallest to shortest; who is in the middle? Is this an average? Move from non standard measures to checking how big kites made from squared paper are. Count the squares, make kites with tails of individual squares. How many do you need?

Averages display

This is a step by step guide to working out averages. There is a pale blue background with a four inch wide black border. Children's work is double mounted with dark and light blue papers. Statements such as: *how to find an average,* are linked by arrows to the next stages.

Averages topic ideas

Do some tin stacking activities. Make rows that decrease one at a time. Can the children work out how many tins will be needed for a stack of a particular height (five, six or ten rows for example)? Ask questions about averages, such as: is the middle row of a stack of odd numbered rows always the average? Do some dice rolling and calculate the average score of twenty rows. Discuss the idea of symmetry in relation to averages and balance. Grow some seedlings, measure them and work out the average. Compare the height and weight of children and make a simple graph (as right). Can you predict how heavy children will be, based on their height?

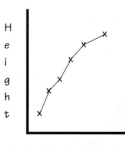

Resources

Patterned fabric, card, beads, baskets, calculators, sticks, counting bricks, abacus, balls, toys, poster paper,

41

Shapes

The shape display

Green poster paper is arranged in a small area leading to the hall. The border is made of green stamped triangles on white. Pictures are mounted on black sugar paper. Include questions such as: how many corners has a cuboid, what shape has four equal sides, what shape are the faces of a cube? Arrange sculptures, mobiles and fabrics printed by children with a few books.

Topic ideas

Print an old cotton sheet using ready mixed paints applied with foam printing pads. Draw around shapes with black paint, colour the shapes to make balanced visual effects. Make shape sculptures from cubes, tubes and balls; paint them. Look at pictures by Cubists, Mondrian and Picasso (see page 79).

Look around the classroom discussing the shapes of things that can be seen. Ask *What shape is the window? What shape is the door? What shape is the clock?* Make a list of things, draw them and note the shapes alongside. Write poems about shapes (link with animals: *the Giraffe is tall and thin, an elephant is round).*

Cut out sets of different plane shapes from differently coloured card. Include triangles, squares and circles. Ask the children to organise the shapes according to colour or shape. Do simple matching activities using three or four simple plane shapes. Make simple patterns from cut gummed paper. Extend this with older children by making Aztec style patterns as below. Use Polydron.

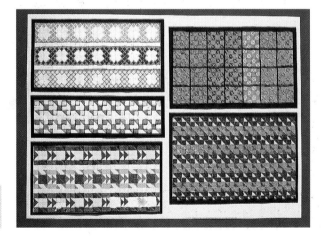

Investigate three dimensional shapes using, Constructastraws, Meccano and Lego.

Use shapes to move things in the classroom. Use strong shapes to make things, emphasise the need to match materials and shapes.

Resources

Green poster paper, black sugar paper, sculptures, mobiles, fabric, cotton sheet, foam printing pads, paints, coloured card, scraps

Exploding shapes display

Brightly coloured exploded abstract shapes (including some hidden faces) are mounted on black and edged in white. Patterned, symmetric and asymmetric geometric designs can contain great variety based on simple elements.

Topic ideas

Give children a choice of different coloured craft papers and ask them to think about which shapes would go with the colours they have chosen. Then, draw carefully and cut out a large bold geometric shape such as square, triangle, circle, rectangle (or some more complex ones). Use containers with many different shapes for printing on paper or fabric (use the ends for this).

Use triangle shaped pieces of coloured paper for tessellation activities. Use boxes and regularly shaped scraps to make three dimensional structures: robots, strange animals or people.

Try this

Chess board: Draw an 8X8 grid of squares like a chess board. How many squares are there? (204) Use different coloured felt tip pens to outline each square.

Cubes: Use grids like the one below. Try drawing cubes or cuboids by joining the dots. Colour parallel faces with the same colour.

Phonics

Clown alphabet display

Design and make an alphabet clown. Cut out from a colourful piece of fabric (the size to suit your room) the outline of a clown. Pad out the area for the head with matching colours and make a pointed hat and a loop for hanging at the top. Using strips of contrasting fabric on which cut out alphabet letters are fixed. Make pockets to hold soft toys. Ask children to bring in their toys, sort them by name and put them in the appropriate pockets with their initials marked on them. The clown can be made stronger by sewing canes or dowel behind the shoulders and above the legs.

Use cross-stitch on Binca to embroider initials. Roll out biscuit pastry, cut out initials and bake. Draw large initials on paper. Trace over with paint, filling in open shapes with colours. Make handwriting patterns with charcoal on newsprint, again complete the pattern with paint.

Our sound this week is 'M'

Display different letters of the alphabet throughout the year; this week the letter is 'M'. A few cut out pictures, models and toys are simply mounted on a light grey background with labels highlighting the initial letters alongside. Simple, large letters at the top emphasise the outline of the letter 'M' and movement directions link the sound with writing.

Use initial letters to build up dictionary skills. Find words beginning with 'M'. Group reception children together who share the same initial. Write down everybody's name and think of some more starting with 'M'. Do some metaphor work, a name starting with 'M' represents a character such as mouse, make 'S' into a snake, tell stories about the characters, make Plasticine models of them, draw pictures of their homes and include as part of the display.

Choose a word from the display such as 'mouse'. Fold A3 paper lengthwise. Open and paint the word 'mouse' on one side of the crease. Fold, rub down, open again and use the pattern as a starting point for painting mouse's house.

Storyland

The display

A bright collection showing children's favourite titles to stimulate imaginative work. Fix lettering from shiny foil diagonally across yellow paper. Get the children to paint pictures of their favourite story characters from books they have brought into school. Double mount the pictures using black and yellow.

Make a flicker book of a scene from a story or a simple action (*Postman Pat* stroking his cat).

Make a word book and write down new words from stories. Choose a favourite story and redesign the front cover. Design a board game based on a story.

The children imagine they work for a children's book company and have to write a précis for the back cover. Write a journal or log for one of the characters in the favourite story.

Rhymes

The display

Young children have tackled D&T problems by making the three Piggies' houses from different materials. The labels are direct and use colours that link with the materials used. Many fairy stories and nursery rhymes can be used in this way.

Other display title ideas
- Secret garden
- The far away tree
- Fantasy island
- Hickory Dickory Dock
- Incey wincey spider
- Jack Sprat could eat no fat
- Rub-a-dub-dub
- Hey diddle diddle
- Humpty Dumpty
- Little Miss Muffet
- Ring-a-ring o' roses
- Three blind mice
- Pat-a-cake, pat-a-cake

An awfully big adventure

The display

Use Art Maché, clay or wood based modelling compound to make small sculptures of Hook, the Croc and other characters from *Peter Pan.* Maps, pictures and written work are mounted on pastel blue paper. The border is a lush mixture of sponge printed greens on white (these colours match the marbled paper used for mounts). The models are finished with Decorlack varnish (NES Arnold).

Topic ideas

 Make individual *Never Never Land* books. Make imaginative cut outs to allow reader to enter the world. Include cut out foliage from magazines.

Change scales. Make small pictures of Peter Pan and enlarge using squared paper.

Try this

Convert a small room into *Never Never Land.* Surround the doorway with paper foliage. Make Hook's ship and fill the room with all kinds of props .

Resources

Clay or wood modelling compcount, Art Mache, Decorlack varnish, squared paper, magazines, paints, scraps

47

Books

Books display

This display is designed to attract interest, give information and prompt questions about books of all kinds. First, make a list of points to be covered. Collect relevant books and write down questions and statements for the labels. Around the black paper backing is a colour stained cartridge paper border (see below). Cut-out lettering for the title is also made from stained paper (use a sandwich of three pieces of paper to cut out three in one go). Mount the books and labels with dressmakers' pins.

Paper for borders, labels and arrows

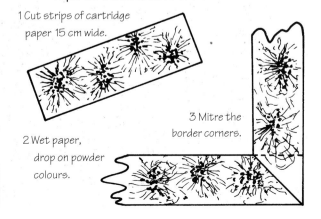

1 Cut strips of cartridge paper 15 cm wide.

2 Wet paper, drop on powder colours.

3 Mitre the border corners.

Topic ideas

This and the following page are about books. The topic ideas are spread on both pages.

Use the display to explore different kinds of books and what makes a good book. Talk about reasons for liking books; for example, characters, words, illustrations and the cover design. Follow up by listening to the particular features that children like in their favourite books.

Try this

Reading restaurant: Children write stories in a structured way, drafting, sharing and redrafting whilst including plots, suspense and building to the climax of the story. When complete, the stories are offered to the 'reading restaurant' (one part of the room). Categorise the stories and put them on a menu according to their content. In the afternoons or when children read together, they can choose from the menu and have a waiter serve them the story of their choice.

DT Design and make books as shown. Use IT to type them up and draw illustrations. Making books can enrich all kinds of topics. The illustrations below show how to make some of these: a giant book, pop up books, folded (extended) books, animal books and simple stitched books.

Pop up books

Giant book

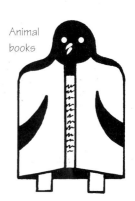

Animal books

Giant

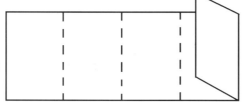

Folded or extending books

Make books the shapes of plants, people or animals, as records of investigations and observations on living things.

Make extending books, as above, for bridges and transport themes. Make costume design books from different periods. Make kings and queens head books. Make silhouette books of famous people made with black card (include written account on reverse of the silhouette picture). Make a pirate's treasure chest book (hinge at the top and the bottom, opening across the middle).

1% +4 Make folded number books for young children that open out as friezes.

Retell the story of Christmas and make a book the shape of the stable or a star. Retell and illustrate the story of *Noah's Ark* or *Joseph's Coat of Many Colours* and the *Wondrous Draught of Fishes*.

Make book of journey to school or record of a school trip. Include maps, records of weather, compass directions, rock types and other environmental features.

Writing & printing display

A time line from 30,000 BC to 1994 wanders across a corner display unit. Artwork, artefacts, hand prints, early clay cuneiform tablets, illuminated hand written text, wax seals and modern typesetting and photographic imagery are linked with a strong caption structure. Prepare the border and title paper (10 cm wide) by marbling or spattering light colours all along it, finish by including hieroglyphs, Greek and Arabic letters, Chinese characters, Morse code symbols and shorthand. The border strip and artwork are then mounted on black and gold papers. The arrows are produced from the same paper and in the way described on page 12. Small shelves are fitted to the display boards to support small artefacts.

This display and *In the news* on the following page, cover different aspects of communications and the topic ideas are presented together.

Writing and printing

In the news display

The display combines some artefacts, such as an old fashion typewriter and quill pens with a selection of stories from newspapers mounted with a border cut from the titles of newspapers. Make up folders containing children's newspapers and collect international newspapers to include in the display. Try to get copies of old newspapers from your record office or library.

Topic ideas

Brainstorm and list all kinds of human communication that you can think of: word of mouth, books, codes, TV, radio, the Internet, newspapers, letters, reports and all types of written materials.

Make clay tablets and use wedge shaped sticks to make cuneiform writing. Make large collage picture of a town crier to include in the display. Read a newspaper story and tell it through a series of cartoon pictures (using no speech and covering all the events).

Make codes to convey secret messages (work in pairs or groups and try to crack each other's codes). Calculate the probability of particular codes being cracked by chance. Use grids to divide pages of newspapers to take headlines, photographs and text.

Write short stories about personal experiences and rewrite as newspaper stories with headlines, subheadings and short paragraphs. Read articles from junior newspapers and then write a letter from *Our correspondent in Toy Town* (or from current international hotspot). Write shape poem about town criers. Write fairy tale newspaper.

Make sound effects and music to accompany a video presentation for class assembly.

Make Plasticine models and use them to tell a story. Video record frame by frame or photograph the models in sequence to tell the story (like a cartoon strip). Design and make code machines as illustrated. Use Lego to make models of early printing presses.

Code machine

1 Cut two discs of card.
2 Mark letters as shown.
3 Fix with paper fastener.
4 Rotate for new codes.

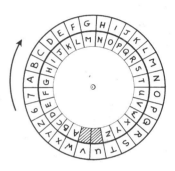

Write newspaper articles and produce a pirate or Victorian newspaper.

Read articles with strong moral elements. Ask the children to imagine that they are characters in the story. Write what they would do in the situations.

Try taking prints from different surfaces. Ask your local printer for some old litho plates, try them, draw on them with lithographic chalks. Wet the plates, roll oil inks across. See the water resist the ink. Try taking prints.

Screen printing display

Screen printing involves squeezing ink or paint through a fabric screen (on which is a stencil of some kind). The ink can be used to print on paper, plastic or fabrics. This display shows the process of screen printing: What we did, what went wrong and what worked. Children's work, equipment, a screen, pair of scissors, transparent stencil sheets, inks, a squeegee and a commentary on what happened are mounted on an oatmeal coloured display board. The main colours are picked up from the flower print which is in red and green. The border is a thick edging of thin red stripes on a thick green strip. The topic ideas on this and the next page are related to all kinds of print-making.

Topic ideas

Try using wax from a batik pen to draw directly onto a screen. When dry, paint over with dilute PVA. Iron the screen between sheets of newsprint to remove the wax, thus producing a stencil, print from it. Make bubble prints by mixing colours and detergent with water in a bowl. Blow air under the surface to produce bubbles. Drop paper onto the surface to take prints.

Use screen printing to print T-shirts with slogans or paper carrier bags to sell for school funds. Write and print posters for special events.

Print with finger paints. Spread paints on clean mixing tray, quickly draw pictures with fingers and place clean paper onto the wet paint, rub down and remove to see monoprint. Cut special card combs (opposite) to use in place of fingers. Print from textured materials: what sort of marks will sponge, a woollen glove or bark make when printed? Try contrasting colours of paper and paint. Make a texture gallery. Do some marbling.

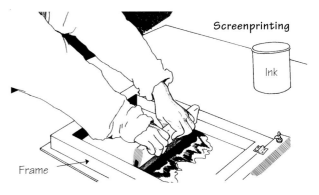

Print making

Blockprinting display

What kind of things are good for printing from? Collect a range of materials, stick them onto printing plates and try them out as shown below. Record the results and make a display as shown.

Topic ideas

There are lots of materials that can be used to print from, such as Lino, polystyrene sheets, clay and corrugated card. Combinations of different materials cut, arranged and glued to a solid base can make attractive and successful printing surfaces. Common to all block printing is the fact that ink or paint is rolled over the printing surface and the protruding parts pick up the ink which then is passed onto the paper or fabric.

Use cold water dyes such as Dylon to print on cotton with a regular pattern from a especially prepared printing block. Use a block made from cut felt shapes stuck onto Lino. Mark the cotton with guidelines for a repeating pattern before printing. Use chalk for the guidelines.

Resources

Polystyrene, Lino, glue, ink or paint, wax, fabric screen, batik pen, transparent stencil sheets, squeegee, corrugated card

card combs

The theatre

The display

The use of golden drapes to frame this corner display immediately gives a flavour of the theatre. It invites people to look inside. The borders and the paper for the lettering have been prepared by spattering gold onto the paper. A puppet theatre (made by children) and hanging changes of scenery are mounted on the display board. There are a number of three dimensional features to the display including beautiful masks in pink and blue, head pieces, large painted papier maché boots and folded and rolled work mounted on black, golden and red, coordinating with the overall scheme.

Topic ideas

Measure faces for masks. As a general guide the eye line is in the middle of the face and the tip of the nose half way between the line of the eyes and the chin. Do a class survey and find out the average positions of features on a face. Measure materials: to make theatres and to cast faces (use Modroc - plaster bandage). Estimate quantities of Art Maché to build up masks. Work out the scale for puppets to fit in the small theatre.

Discuss famous characters or read stories about the theatre, pantomime, the circus and write a class book about the theatre. Rewrite pantomimes and present as a school play.

Notice the changes in plaster (Modroc) as it hardens and heats up while curing.

Write and record sound effects and music to synchronise with a puppet performance.

Put on a performance of an Ancient Greek play. Use pictures and other source material to produce a book about the history of the theatre. Make copies of dramatic masks and shadow puppets.

Design and make puppet theatres as shown below. Design and make sets for school plays (see page 7). Use a wooden frame and old sheet to make shadow theatre. Use ethnic shadow puppets and make some card silhouette characters.

Make different kinds of masks: painted, face surrounds, paper plate, papier maché built up masks, balloon masks and masks made from old painted cardboard boxes. Cast children's face masks, using Modroc. Make puppets.

Resources

Modroc, pencils, paints, brushes, palettes, scissors, paper plates, card, string (for fixing masks), Art Maché

Shakespeare

The display

A stencilled foliage border on an oatmeal coloured strip surrounds black backing paper. The title lettering is cut from white and mounted on buff paper. Reproductions of portraits of Shakespeare and his home are mixed with children's work to give a history of the bard. Cut out carefully decorated characters from *The Tempest* are fixed to the display board. Masks and old pewter tankard, dancing shoes and books are arranged in front.

Topic ideas

Role play what life was like in Tudor times or make a tableau of four scenes. Make costumes for a production of a rewritten play. Make a timeline of important events since Shakespeare. Work in groups of six (a priest, peasant, teacher, King, servant and courtier). Find out what life was like for these people and tell the class.

Try this

A writing project: This is designed to help story work over a period of ten lessons. 1 Each child chooses a special person to write for (parent, friend). Discuss the kind of story (book) that this person might like. For homework, find out. 2 Bring in favourite story and discuss its good features. 3 Work with a partner to draft own story including i) Title; ii) Opening sentence; iii) The characters; iv) Leading to the climax; v) The ending. Children should talk to their partner about their outline story and ask questions. 4 Write their first paragraph of the story without worrying too much about spelling and punctuation. Have some good examples of beginnings available to look at. 5 Concentrate on the start of the story working closely with the partner, sharing ideas and redrafting. 6 Continue with the beginning of the story. 7 Children concentrate on the build up to the climax with suspense, subplots and meaning. 8 Read a number of well known climaxes from stories. Children discuss the different features of their stories and write their own climax. 9 In pairs review and improve stories. 10 Read some endings. Children finish their story.

Diwali

The display

The main colours in this display are red, purple and gold, combined with white and gold diaphanous fabrics. The purple backing paper is edged with a gold edged black border. Brilliantly coloured ethnic cloths are combined with Mehndi hands, script and Diwali images. The artwork is double mounted using matching colours and in the foreground are some Diwali lamps made by the children.

Topic ideas

The importance of light as a religious idea crosses many cultures. The topic ideas extend beyond religion in a cross-curricular way.

Discuss the importance of light and how it must be difficult to be blind. In the playground, when there are no obstructions, lead the class blindfold carefully, exploring the wide open spaces. Safety is very important in this activity. Ask the children to write about their experience and how the absence of light can be linked with ignorance and a sense of being lost. Read stories about light such as *The Lighthouse Keeper's Lunch*. Retell the story with illustrations. Invent words for different types of light and do a word search, perhaps even a quiz about light, checking the spelling. Look through a telescope and write about what they see.

Use sunlight to tell the time (shadow clocks), compare with candle clocks.

Find out about celebrations of light such as Christmas, Hannuka, Candlemass and the Orthodox Easter. Visit places of worship and list the kinds of light that can be found (candles, stained glass windows, natural light arranged to fall in special places).

Make candles and candle holders for a display. Using candle light make and cut out silhouettes. Make star mobiles. Use coloured acetate and black card to make stained glass windows.

Design and make a lighthouse from scraps, batteries and light bulbs. Design and make candle holders and decorative stars for different festivals.

Find out how light changes during the seasons and record the day lengths once a week for a season. Make a plan of the school and go on a walk around the school, locating and mapping all of the light sources.

Brainstorm ideas: where does light come from? Why is it brighter at some times of the day? What is night? Discuss other light sources and make a simple electric circuit to make a light flash. Use prisms and reflective materials to investigate light. How far away is the sun? What makes the moon shine? Set up some experiments to see how strong light affects coloured materials by fading them. Set up experiments to check the effect of light on young plants.

Make a time line of when and how different forms of lighting have been discovered/used. Talk about myths and legends of fire and light.

Firework night

The display

Ten or twelve shiny bright drawings on black or dark purple paper double and triple mounted make an explosive bonfire night display. The mounts are combinations of brown, black, cream and dark blue. They are dynamically arranged from the centre of a silver backing. In the middle, the title is presented. The top part of the display contains all kinds of fireworks whizzing around, spirals of floating coloured paper and rockets.

Topic ideas

This display links with the *Diwali* display on the previous page and the *Christmas advent* display on page 59.

Collect as much information about Guy Fawkes as possible and try to sequence the story. Why did Guy Fawkes want to blow up parliament? What happened as a result? Compare with current affairs that shock nations.

Class activity, circle time (class sit in a circle and roll ball across to choose speaker). Speak on current issues of national importance. Write Guy Fawkes diary.

Talk about individual children's rights and responsibilities, class rules, bullying, making reasoned arguments. Can terrorism be justified?

Try this

A moving debate: Divide the class and debate *Guy Fawkes- Was he right or wrong?* See page 15.

Diamond statements: Teacher makes twelve plausible statements about Guy Fawkes. Make a diamond grid on the blackboard with one box at the top, then two, and three, then declining to one again. Children sort statements from top to bottom according to priority of importance.

Birthdays

Happy birthday display

A light blue backing paper with enormous white and pink bordered lettering is decorated with cut out self-portraits, red, pink and blue balloons, wrapped up birthday presents, birthday cards, a cake, favourite button badges and a class *Happy Birthday* book.

Topic ideas

Discuss birthdays, special ones, the zodiac and birthday celebrations in different countries.

Make a timeline of special events in a child's life. Ask grandparents to come in and talk about life when they were children and how they celebrated their birthdays.

Make birthday cards and a make believe birthday cake, print wrapping paper. Make a train calendar frieze with carriages to hold little pictures of each child as shown below.

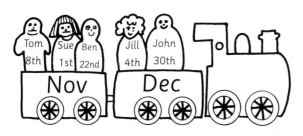

In which month were most children born? Make a graph showing the frequency of birthdays throughout the months.

Do birds and animals get born at particular times of the year and why? Arrange a visit of a newborn baby; what can babies do themselves?

Italian nativity display

Mount reproductions of famous nativity scenes on black paper and then on a gold background. A matching gold border adds to the overall image.

Topic ideas

Look at and discuss the pictures. Talk about motherhood, love and peace. Use the paintings as starting points for creative writing and children's own paintings.

Resources

Gold paper and border, 24 red candles, PVA, silver paint, bucket of sand, presents, pictures, wrapping papers, balloons, paints

Advent calendar display

Make up Christmas tree using shiny green material with twenty four red candles, one for each day of the advent. Make two sets of flames from gold and silver foil (or paper), one on top of the other acting as a cover to be removed. The top set of flames have numbers 1 to 24 to be removed one a day, while the bottom set is fixed on the tree and is decorated with Christmas images. As the cover candle flames are taken off, fix them along the top of the display as shown. Children's letters and pictures sent to Father Christmas are also displayed with presents, Christmas cards and books.

Topic ideas

 Make Christmas cards by dripping PVA glue onto folded card and then spray with silver paint. Make Christmas decorations. Use a dry branch of a tree, stand it in a bucket of sand, spray with paint and decorate with small presents for every child. Use clay and other materials to make a nativity scene.

 Discuss the kinds of materials that would be suitable to make swaddling clothes for Jesus.

Write Joseph's diary of events leading to Christmas. Write the story from another point of view. How did Herod see things? Write a story about the phrase: light at the end of the tunnel.

Make stars, camels and gifts as part of a tableau.

What is the importance of Christmas? Jesus is The Light of the World for Christians. Have periods of quiet 'stilling time' and light a candle. Discuss the differences between gifts and talents.

Make another display featuring the three Kings and present a verse from the carol as a tableau. Each group presents one verse and children act as characters or props.

Make a map of the journey to Bethlehem. Discuss the way that Christmas is celebrated around the world.

The display

The Wilton Diptych is one of the most famous examples of Western art. It is an English royal portrait as well as a religious icon. It shows Richard II with his patron saints who recommend him to Mary. It is interesting that the angels wear the king's badge, the white hart and peascod collar. This exquisite portrait shows Richard's love of art and contrasts with his own brutal murder; civilisation flew in through one window and out another.

Displays do not have to be in Technicolour to be effective. This impressive display combines dark blues and gold with the colours of a rich collection of natural materials. Framed reproductions of the Diptych are mounted with children's versions and written work. The mounts for the children's work are carefully produced using gold patterned paper. Miniature icons and wooden models of a church tower reinforce the religious atmosphere.

The Wilton Diptych

Medieval crafts

Topic ideas

 Use materials that were available to medieval artists. Try using traditional wood glue and painting with egg tempera.

Make illuminated manuscripts with large decorative letters and floral borders. Cut patterned paper as shown below to form lettering from displays. Copy medieval portraits and paint on prepared panels. Use plywood board if authentic materials are not available. Use a variety of materials including oil paints. Invite a technician from an art college or secondary school to demonstrate the use of traditional artists' materials. Use foil craft materials to produce gold effect patterned backing for icons. Use metallic paints to produce gilded effects. Make stencils (see page 60).

Visit medieval sites, particularly monasteries, abbeys and old churches.

 Discuss why kings and queens wanted to be in pictures that included Jesus and the virgin Mary. Does this happen in other religions? Is it morally acceptable? Make a list of the different kinds of religious art, statues, icons, mosaics, tapestries, paintings, manuscripts and of course architecture.

Listen to medieval music, such as the Gregorian chants and recordings of authentic medieval instruments. Do a performance of plainsong.

Use a medieval picture as the starting point for role play or story writing.

Resources

Wooden panels, plywood, eggs, pigments, pestle and mortar, brushes, foil craft sheets, metallic papers

Seasons

The displays

Spring, summer and autumn, winter

Cover two square display boards with triangular pieces of paper as backgrounds to the seasons. Use blue and yellow for summer and spring, red and green for autumn and winter. Use yellow lettering for the spring display and blue, red and green for the other seasons. Colour theme each section, for example, cut out green and red holly to border the winter area and use yellow flowers on the spring background colour. Mount the work on single black mounts and add dried flowers, grasses, leaves and craft paper flowers.

Topic ideas

The topic ideas are spread over this and the next page as the displays are interconnected.

Look at four pictures showing the differences in the seasons. Note the physical changes. Use the pictures as discussion points, for example,

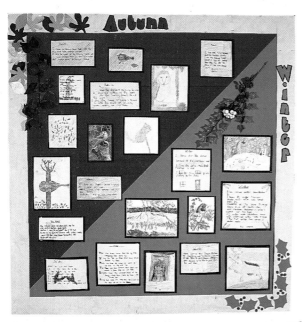

discuss snow, ice, the changes in materials such as water as it freezes and bread as it is toasted to warm us up. Observe and draw twigs as they bud in the spring, plant bulbs as they develop. In the spring, do a mini topic on the colour green. Make bird cake from seed to put on a bird table. Make and use compost to sow seeds. Look at colours, shapes, smell and taste of fruits. In wet weather, go into the playground and name the puddles you find. Measure and draw around them with chalk. Note changes to the shape and the size of them as the weather changes. Try to estimate the amount of water that was contained in the puddles. Check the estimates by pouring measured amounts of water onto the puddle space until the original outline is matched.

Resources

Coloured papers, card, dried flowers, leaves, fabric, fruits, seeds, construction toys, compost, clay, Plasticine

Write stories about *Where Henry has gone*, and acrostic puddle poems. Use creative writing about apples, hedgerows, squirrels, hibernation, migration of birds, hedgehogs, harvest, corn and bread. Write Christmas and Easter stories and poems. Use simple reportive writing in the topic book.

Write a diary of the countryside. Study the way that seasonal changes have affected people differently over the years, for example, the introduction of central heating and double glazing.

Make classroom friezes for the seasons. Make picture for each season and make two and three dimensional snow flakes. Make collages of snowmen, squirrels, birds such as the robin, and scarecrows. Make cards for Mother's Day, Easter and Christmas. Make calendars and crackers. Make Halloween masks, clay and Plasticine models of animals and small nativity scenes. Make handprint hedgehogs. Make prints from leaves and fruit (try dye printing on fabric). Make hot and cold pictures as shown.

Collect different leaves, seeds and other seasonal items. Set and sort these according to colour, shape and size. Make simple diagrams of three or four stages of development from seeds to plants. Use these for sequencing activities. Compare different seeds by measuring sizes and shapes and by weighing (conkers, hazelnuts, sunflower seeds). Match different shapes. Make stick graphs for rain, sunshine and temperature.

Brainstorm the changes in the seasons and link this activity with the changes children experience as they grow. Discuss the influence of weather on living things and human beings (health, feelings, friendliness, exposure to sunlight). Keep weather charts, make a diary of the weather. Discuss changes brought about by global warming. How can we halt environmental damage?

Discuss ideas of renewal, birth, death and the need for awareness and concern for each other and other living things. Sing seasonal hymns such as *We plough the field and scatter.*

Design and make:

- a model snow mover (with large construction toys),
- a plant pot for seeds,
- a bag to carry fruit home in from the shops,
- lemon shaped and flavoured biscuits,
- an instrument for recording the rainfall.

Try this

Storm: Discuss composing a piece of music about a storm. Write ideas on board for reference. One child will direct the whole piece, whilst the others choose instruments to make the sounds of hail, wind, rain, followed by sunshine. They have to agree signs for louder, softer, pitch, dynamics and timbre. Spend two sessions of twenty minutes preparing for the performance and then tape record the performance which should last about twenty minutes.

63

Wind power

Speech bubbles in display:
Joseph and Etienne Montgolfier were two French brothers.

In 1783 they made the first hot air balloon.

the first balloon flight

The balloon was royal blue and gold. Here are our designs:~

In our topic books we have written the story of the Montgolfier balloon flight.

A duck, a sheep and a cockerel flew two miles in eight minutes.

Balloons display

This is a simple, but very effective small wall display. Colours do not have to be bright and garish to be effective. A feature of the use of colour in this display is the way that the white and blue striped backing fabric is picked up again and used for the double mounting of the children's work. In the mounts, the stripes are horizontal to contrast with the vertical stripes on the background. The fabrics are separated slightly by the use of a thin black double mounting edge. Cloud shaped speech bubbles in tones of blue and white contain information in a jolly way. Vertical and horizontal appliqué pictures of balloons colour theme beautifully using gold, blues and black as decorative elements in the balloon designs. The *First balloon flight* title lettering is cut from shiny gold material, and goes off across the black border, taking the display into the classroom itself.

Topic ideas

 Draw nine large balloons on a piece of paper. Divide each balloon into three parts. Use only three colours and make as many different colour combinations as possible.

Make a balloon batik wall hanging. Use balloons and papier maché to make masks.

Try this

Balloon machine: The task is to design and make a machine which is wind powered. It must have at least one part that can be moved by a jet of air. Get the children to work with specific materials only. Balloons, paper, card, cocktail sticks, drawing pins, plastic bottle nozzles, rubber bands, glue and Selotape can be used. The balloon can provide the jet of air and once started the machine should not need to be touched again. Before starting work ask questions like: How many ways can air be used to move things? What sort of weight can be moved by air power? For how long can machines operate? What is a fair test for success?

Work in pairs. Design and make the machines and test them. Add designs to the balloons. Record the results.

See illustrations opposite and page 65 for this.

Balloon machine

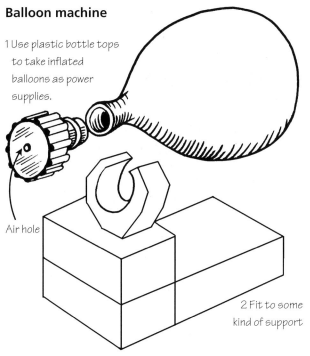

1 Use plastic bottle tops to take inflated balloons as power supplies.

Air hole

2 Fit to some kind of support

Windy days display

The background is a buff coloured sugar paper onto which is fixed a silhouette of a tree, cut from black paper. To cut out such a large tree you need to:

1 measure the paper to fit the display board,
2 work on the reverse of the paper using a light coloured chalk to sketch the outline (doing this will avoid marking the front of the tree),
3 cut out the silhouette carefully,
4 turn the paper over and fix to the display board.

Sort out fabrics, papers and natural materials such as acorns and leaves. With the children choose the appropriate materials for the different parts of the display. Work with children in small groups. Some can make up elements such as leaves cut from different coloured craft papers (brown and tones of green), some can paint fir cones and seeds with metallic and other colours whilst others with adult help can make up flowers using tissue paper. To make up the figure with the umbrella:

- Sketch out on a large piece of white paper the figure and umbrella.
- Outline the main parts such as the hat, coat, skirt, boots and umbrella with clean felt tip lines.
- Cut them out and use them as a pattern to make up the coloured parts which you assemble on the display.

Try this

Turbine for the balloon machine: Design and make a turbine for the balloon machine. Use paper for the turbine blades to make sure they are light enough to be blown around. You can use card to make strong supporting parts for the turbine blades. Discuss design ideas, experiment and test the results. Try to make the designs look attractive and realistic, by adding colours and patterns to the turbine blades.

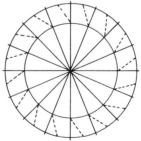

Sample turbine design

Resources

Balloons, paper, card, cocktail sticks, leaves, plastic bottle nozzles, fabric, rubber bands, Selotape, chalk, drawing pins

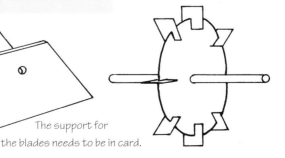

Turbine blades must be made of paper so that they are light enough to be blown around.

The support for the blades needs to be in card.

Favourite foods display

Get the children to use Plasticine or wood based modelling material to make their favourite food. Get them to make plates of food and colour them carefully. Use a lightly striped wallpaper as background. Place a folded tablecloth on top and put the food and the captions in position. Use coloured lettering for the title and edge the whole display board with children's stencilled images of food. Add questions to the display related to healthy eating and balanced diet.

Topic ideas

Discuss healthy eating in connection with favourite foods. Why do adults give children sweets? Make a visit to the supermarket, list low fat foods and bring in from home labels and cereal cartons. Read poems such as *Jack Sprat could eat no fat* and ask the children to write a story about what happened to the Sprat family, assuming they did not change their diet. Do an unscrambled game of ten naturally sweet foods: *'pleaps, snrapsip, gifs, resunp, torcars, sraep, mulps, siarins, edats and gnroaes'.*

Make a diary of food eaten during the week. Break it in categories of fat, carbohydrate, protein and fibre. Use cereal packets and compare the kinds of additives included. Ask questions: *What foods are added to muesli to make it sweet? What does it mean if it says on the packet 'no added sugar'? What fibre foods are contained in the cereals?*

Do a survey of what people eat for breakfast (use tally charts). Include these categories: no breakfast, drink only, continental, cereal, cereal+, cooked and other (fruit, for example). Make a pictogram of the fat, fibre, sugar, salt and calories contained in typical servings (30-60 grams) of a range of cereals. Use things like chocolate bars to do work on fractions. Link this to fractions of circles and other simple shapes. Do a survey of what is the ideal dinner from health and personal choice.

Talk about celebration foods and symbols such as the bread of life. Discuss the importance of fasting in many religions.

Food for living

Thank you for the food we eat display

Get children to make models of themselves as chefs, using cut out face shapes, paints and glue. Make their own designs of meals on plates and make three dimensional arms to hold the plates away from the display board. Mount other meals on plate settings and combine all the elements on the display board, fixing firmly. Discuss with the children and make a list of words that they want to say about foods. Use these as labels, some coming from the chef's mouth. Stencil the border, using a biscuit shaped design.

Topic ideas

Make a trip to a farm and study the field patterns, making notes on the crops that are grown. Make a map of the trip to the farm and include the information about crops on it. Do full day simulation games such as *World harvest game* and *Why people go hungry* (Oxfam). Get photographs of different European farming environments such as Rhone valley, Greek olive groves and a Scottish salmon river. Find out what kinds of foods are produced in the different European Union countries and compare these with a Tanzanian village (see *Living and learning in a Tanzanian village,* published by DEP, Manchester development education project, c/o Manchester Polytechnic). Discuss the kind of weather needed for growing different crops and list those produced locally and others that are imported.

Make collages and paintings based on the field pattern systems (or try small ceramic patterned tiles). Use food to print on fabrics with Dylon dyes. Make drawings of farmers at work and animals in the fields.

Resources

Blue poster paper, white edging strip, paper plates, card, grey sugar paper, scrap materials, silver paper

Buon appetito!

Foods and packs display

Collect cereal boxes, pasta, lentils and other dried food stuff. The display includes children's work made from typical contents of the boxes arranged as landscapes, field patterns or abstract designs (contact supermarkets for foods which are beyond their shelf life). Simply glue the food stuffs in place on the backing papers (or card). When dry, mount and arrange with the cereal boxes.

Topic ideas

Discuss the way that colours are used in advertising and how packaging relies on efficient use of materials which are often transformed from two dimensional nets into 3D shapes. Design and make:

- a label for an amazing new fizzy drink,
- packaging for eggs to be sent through the post,
- packaging for bananas to be used as display and transporting of the fruit,
- alternative packaging for strawberries.

Make lists of fresh fruit and preserved food. How would people's health be affected if only preserved food was available. Talk about the importance of vitamins to health and make a chart of the best sources of the main vitamins.

Measure cereal boxes, work out the volume of the contents. Open them out, measure the nets and work out the area of card used to contain specific volumes/weights of foods. Which are the most efficient shapes to use for cartons?

Italian food display

Children's impressions of Italian paintings of food are mounted on single black mounts. These and the reproductions of paintings are fixed on a light blue pastel background which is surrounded by blue marbled paper. The title is cut out from border paper and mounted on black paper. In front of the display board, garlic, chianti and muslin bags of pasta are arranged.

Topic ideas

Read about life in Italy and other countries. Write and design cafe menus. Include prices in local currencies.

Find out what kinds of meal a typical Italian family would have during the day and compare with British families.

Arrange an Italian feast. Choose and cook Italian food Including salads, pizza, pasta and maybe home-made ice cream.

Link this topic with Romans on page 72.

Jingle Jangle Scarecrow

The display

This farm concert display features children's models of animals together with the sounds they make and a mobile of the Jingle Jangle scarecrow. The display board is covered with a light beige colour with a stencilled border. The Jingle Jangle scarecrow has his body parts labelled and he and some sheep are hanging from the ceiling with coat hangers. The children's work includes pictures of the scarecrow, little pigs and graphs showing favourite animals. The models are mounted behind the front frieze of green cut out paper to represent grass. Photographs of farming in the past and artifacts complete the display. The scarecrow is made from old clothes and fabrics stuffed with straw.

Topic ideas

Make a visit to a museum or farm. Prepare by discussing three and four field systems, rotations of crops and the kind of crops grown many years ago. What was the medieval diet like?

Do some phonics work using rhymes such as *Old McDonald* and *Baa baa black sheep*. Write stories and poems about favourite animals and scarecrows.

Resources

Cereal boxes, pasta, pulses, glue, paper, card, scrap materials, spoons, cups, bowls, cardboard boxes, saucepans

Use a model of a farm including different things like the farmhouse, horses, chickens and pigs. Give each one a price such as 50p for a horse and ask the children to choose what they could buy for £5.00. Set problems based on farming such as: Mr. Seed is a farmer. He planted 360 potatoes in one field and 29 fewer in his other field. How many potatoes did he plant all together? If a loaf costs 60p how many can be bought for £3.00? Use field patterns and shapes to introduce fractions and later on percentages. Link this to other shapes such as circles. Bring in some foods such as potatoes and carrots and use for weighing and measuring activities. Cook some; how many can a kilogram of potatoes feed? Compare non standard measures by using spoons, cups, bowls and saucepans for measuring milk and other ingredients in recipes. How long does it take to cook a cake? How long does it take to grow beans or potatoes?

Investigate the way that plants grow under different conditions. Where do plants get their food from? Why do farmers use fertiliser? Use some in experiments.

Discuss animal welfare. For older children, organise a debate. Read Bible stories, for example *Jesus as a shepherd*.

Make scarecrow music using home made instruments. Make the following instruments:
- Shoe box guitar (rubber bands stretched over).
- Paper towel horn. Cover one end of roll with waxed paper held by rubber band, punch holes along roll and sing tunes into open end.
- Tambourines. Staple two paper plates together around the rims, make holes and attach bells.

Egypt

The displays

Living and dead

Make small mummified figures from Modroc clay or plaster. Embalm them and wrap in bandage. Make sarcophagi from wood or cardboard and decorate. Make clay slab models of ancient Egyptian houses. Display the mummies and coffins with books and mount on red background with black border.

Tutankhamen

Discuss ideas of life after death, decay, preservation and changes to materials. Read books and talk about the curse of Tutankhamen. Make a papier maché central feature with two serpents on the head. Include written work, for example from Howard Carter writing to his grandmother explaining about all the wonderful things he has found. Use metallic blues, silvers and gold to reinforce the image of the golden pharaoh. Invent a board game about pyramids.

Write a story about the death of the pharaoh and produce it using hieroglyphics as a newspaper. Practise writing simple hieroglyphics.

Compare Roman and Egyptian numerals. Build pyramids with marbles (three sides on the base). How many marbles are there on each layer? Use Blutack for bigger pyramids.

Topic ideas

Make clay figures. Dip in PVA and wrap bandages around to embalm. Make coffins and pyramids with secret passages (with viewing points). Make collages of Bast the god cat. Make houses from slabs of clay, cutting shapes for steps, windows and doors. Use slip to join parts together.

Imagine finding treasure in a pyramid. Write about it and make some. Discuss Egyptian ideas of life after death and what was needed to take on the journey. Link with Christian ideas of life after death and the notion that it is easier for a camel to pass through the eye of a needle than for a rich man to go to heaven.

Ancient Greece

Resources

Modroc or plaster, clay, bandages, wood or cardboard, paints, craft paper, PVA, papier maché, Greek coins

The display

This wall display contains all kinds of work. A dark blue background is edged by a black border strip stamped with a blue paint motif pattern. Five masks with curled paper hair and beards are mounted above the display board. Drawings of classical buildings, embroidered classical motifs, urn designs, modern Greek coins, fragments of pots and diaries of *A day at the British Museum* complete the display.

Topic ideas

Make red and black ceramic ware, use clay or cut out craft paper. Make masks (as above or using clay) based on traditional tragic designs. Design posters for Olympic games.

Look at pictures and read about the twelve Gods (of Olympus) of Ancient Greece and write about the ways they were similar to human beings.

Try these

Greek key and spirals: the ancient Greek key design is based on a spiral pattern. As spirals grow the sides grow in a regular way. Can children predict how many cubes are needed for the 6th and 10th shapes in the series (see below)? Use interlocking cubes (Multi-link) for this activity and the one below.

Olympic podiums: Can children estimate how many cubes are needed for the 5th, 10th or 50th podium? Build some and check.

Podiums

How many cubes do you need for the 10th or 50th podium? Can you work out a rule?

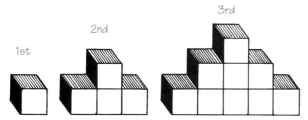

1st   2nd   3rd

Greek key spirals

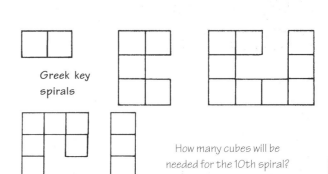

How many cubes will be needed for the 10th spiral?

Romans in Britain

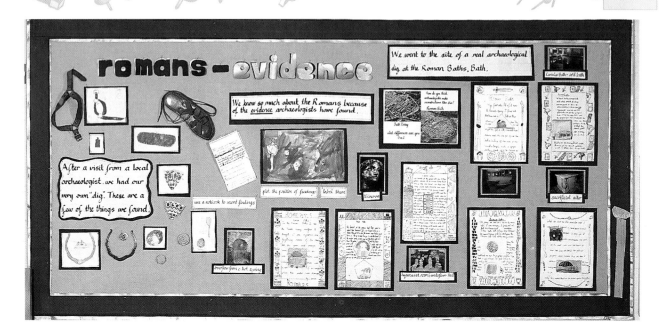

Evidence display

This display contains work from three activities:
- a visit of an archaeologist to the school,
- results of children's own archaeological dig,
- a review of a class visit to a Roman site in Bath.

Use black and gold cut out letters for titles. Mount labels and work on black card. Collect evidence and record it. Write up and illustrate findings. Why not try to make a Roman temple, as well?

The temple

Convert a corner of a classroom into a temple. Use corrugated card to support the pediment (which can be decorated with paints). Make a shrine for the Emperor by mounting his bust on a plinth covered with marbled paper. Hidden lighting will make the Emperor's bust look mysterious.

Topic ideas

Make a timeline across the ceiling from the old Stone Age to Roman times. Ask children to find out what jobs the Gods had. Neptune was the god of...? Jupiter the god of...? Discuss why the Romans left Britain and what evidence of their influence still remains.

Using Roman numerals, do maths on slates. Fold and cut paper into rectangles and use as simple mosaics.

Write about what the Romans and Britons thought about the invasion of England (a letter home from a legionnaire). Discuss the means of transport used by the Romans, make chariots.

Model roads, houses and hypocaust (compare with electricity). Make murals and mosaics.

Use maps and plot Roman towns across Britain. Are Roman roads still in use?

Tudors

The displays

Tudor portraits display

Look at paintings by Holbein and other court painters. Paint portraits of Tudor characters. Make Tudor rose borders as shown and mount with alternating colour background, red and yellow as shown and matching golden letters for the titles. Include questions in the display such as: Only the rich had their portrait painted; why?

Mini corner display

Stain some paper with a brown colour wash to make it look old. With pencil draw a rectangle inside the paper so that a decorative border can be painted around information about Henry the VIII. Try using large initial letters as shown. Paint elliptical miniatures and make small collage pictures of landscapes. Mount with sombre colours.

Topic ideas

 Make a Tudor family tree from Henry VII to Elizabeth. Try to visit the Mary Rose in Portsmouth and make drawings and notes about the famous ship. Discuss what Tudor life was like, dress up in costumes and use role play activities to research and relive the period.

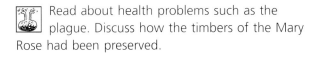 Read about health problems such as the plague. Discuss how the timbers of the Mary Rose had been preserved.

Design and make a machine for raising the Mary Rose. Design and make mazes.

How do people like to be painted? Work in pairs to paint idealised miniatures of each other. Try using different kinds of paints: use oils and paints made with eggs (arrange for a local artist to demonstrate egg tempera methods). Use ready mixed paints with a touch of washing up liquid to paint a gallery on windows (the washing up liquid will make it easy to clean off). Make portraits of Henry and Elizabeth, try using padded appliqué as an alternative to painting. Make clay pin dolls of Tudor characters. Use these as stimulus to role playing. Make miniature paintings or drawings of Tudor people to include in a visual family tree.

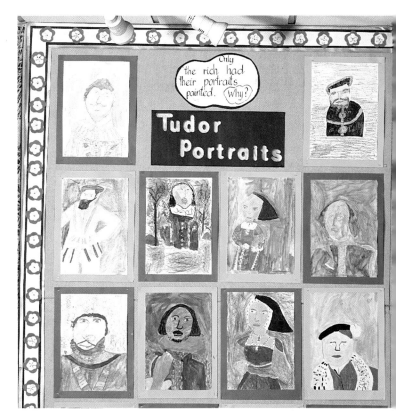

The 1940's

Dear Mother display

This is an evocative display that is colour themed using the colours of the Union Jack together with black and brown. The display is made up of: illustrated letters from homesick evacuated children, models of the old vicarage and other country cottages, paintings of the view from the train during the journey, ration books, gas masks, model aeroplanes, school cap and intertwining foliage. The brown backing paper is edged with pastel blue sugar paper and a wide border of floral wallpaper. The artwork and letters use the blue and wallpaper combined with black card as double or triple mounts. Discuss the role of women at wartime.

Topic ideas

 Write poems: A mother sees..., A soldier sees..., A general sees..., A child sees... Write illuminated letters home from evacuees and soldiers in the front line. Get children to find from older relatives a real wartime story, write and illustrate. Read the stories to class and choose one as a play.

Talk about keeping secrets and invent some codes using numbers and letters.

 Starting with ration books, find out about wartime diets, rationing, waste (the *Squander Bug)* and digging for victory and self-sufficiency.

Design and make an Anderson shelter for the home corner in the classroom. Make a huge wartime computer from cardboard boxes.

Try this

Conrad's war (**Andrew Davies, Hippo**): This book can provide a fascinating range of activities. The following suggestions are made chapter by chapter. First read the prologue and ask the class what are their first impressions of Conrad. Read the play script. What impressions are formed about the family? How realistic is it? **Chapter one:** Write a version of the letter Conrad's dad received from the BBC. Use flash cards and write a sentence of six or seven words including those that the children need to spell, show for 15 seconds and get them to write them down. **Chapter two:** Role play family in groups arguing over the war.

Chapter three: Why does Conrad think that boys don't make dolls? Write instructions on how to build a tank. **Chapter four:** Work in pairs, create flicker books describing events of chapter. **Chapter five:** Ask about remembered dreams, write about. **Chapter six:** Ask children to predict what will happen in next chapter, work in pairs and write their version. **Chapter seven:** Draw a plan of the Lancaster bomber cockpit, make pilot's log of incidents. **Chapter nine:** Make a detailed puppet of Scarface. **Chapter twelve:** Divide A4 page into twelve sections, use pictures and phrases to retell chapter (make sound effects). **Chapter thirteen:** Make *Escape from Colditz* board game. Rewrite ending.

Friend or foe?

This display is inspired by a review of the book by Michael Morpurgo. It includes cut out carefully decorated characters and model aeroplanes hung as mobiles with written work and artwork, double mounted on a black background. Other ideas for wartime displays could include:

- designing and making machines for testing blackout material,
- making an improved garden air-raid shelter
- a display based on wartime songs such as *We'll meet again*.

1940s Wall hanging

Design wall hangings and choose one that combines most elements of the period. Use this as a plan for a large appliqué. Divide up the design into small patterns so that all children are involved. Use hessian, paper, fabrics, straw, wool, clay for medals, flags and corrugated paper.

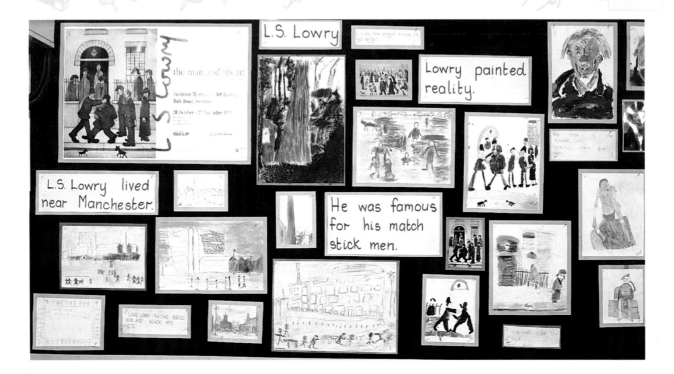

Lowry display

This display includes information about the artist and his life. Children's artwork in pencil, watercolour and charcoal are put alongside some reproductions which inspired their work.

Topic ideas

🏛 Read about the history of the industrial regions of the country and the difficulties of life (unemployment, poverty, poor health) during the 1930s and today. Compare Lowry's pictures with photographs of the Jarrow march and other important events of the period. Write an account with a map of the journey from Jarrow to London.

📖 Write a letter of appreciation to the painter about his work. Pretend that the children are art critics and invite them to write a criticism of Lowry's work for the local paper. Use IT for the articles. Write Haiku poems to express moods of sadness, happiness and quietness.

✏ Look at Lowry's portraits of people and get the children to make pictures of their friends or parents using similar materials. Make drawings of children in the playground using his style. Make studies of industrial scenes.

Display for an awkward place

The illustration above shows how drawings and writing can be mounted in ways that will fit unusual or difficult areas of your classroom. The main thing to remember is to cut pieces of paper first for children to work on, which will actually fit the triangles or odd shaped areas that are available. Careful planning and use of mounts can give a feeling of space.

Add some colour

Colour mixing display

This wall display reinforces the processes of mixing colours. Red and blue make purple, red and yellow make orange, black and white make grey, blue and yellow make green and red and white make pink. The labels which are combined with the children's mixed colours are themselves made from letters which are coloured accordingly. The light blue backing paper is set off with a striking black and white border. The samples of mixed colours and labels are cut out in simple cloud shapes and double mounted on white and black paper.

Topic ideas

List the names of colours such as: brown, red, yellow, blue, green, orange, purple and other less common names for older children such as: turquoise, primrose yellow and violet. Match words with mixed colours or cut paper.

Use rollers to print large rainbow pictures. Try water soluble colour pencils for rainbows, apply water after drawing the design to make the colours blend. Paint pictures of animals and insects showing camouflage and patterns. Marble white paper two or three times to build up mixtures of colour. Divide a paper into six or seven strips. Start from one side with dark blue (or other colour) and add a white to the basic colour in increasing amounts across the strips. Use wet paper and apply washes of colour to produce atmospheric landscapes.

Make a class book on Noah's ark or Joseph's coat of many colours. Make a point of mixing a rich range of colours for the animals in the ark and images of landscapes during the storm and when the rainbow appeared in the sky.

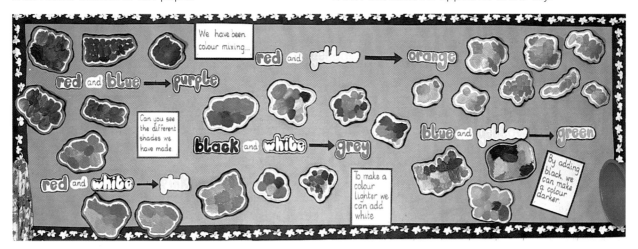

Collect various opaque, transparent and translucent coloured materials. Use these to make collages by overlaying with PVA to produce glazed transparent colour effects. This technique is good for subjects such as *Under the sea,* as shown opposite. Make stained glass type windows:

- On thin typing or tracing paper make a design with heavily applied black crayon. The black lines are like the lead of stain glass windows.
- Colour in between the black lines with bright wax crayons.
- When the design is complete, turn it over and use cotton wool to rub vegetable oil onto the back of the design. Oil makes it transparent.
- Mount on window to see the effect.

Subtle designs

Inspired by William Morris

A border strip of stencilled brown wrapping paper is combined with a fine line of delicately coloured floral paper. A soft pastel blue backing paper is covered with single and double mounted examples of Morris's wallpaper and fabric designs accompanied by the children's developments of the ideas. The double mounts in black and white are sometimes reversed so that the white is inside the black. Allow elements to overlap to add interest to the display. The title lettering is cut from patterned paper.

The Pre-Raphaelites

Something of the story of the Brotherhood is presented in this wall display that is a companion to the one of William Morris. Written work with impressions of Ophelia by Millais are placed in an imaginative way. A watercolour box, paints and brushes give a three dimensional feel to the wall display. Some of the written work is pinned carefully so that it bulges out adding extra interest.

The labels are cut out in soft cloud shapes and are mounted with a thin outline of black. The colours in the reproductions, rose and russet, match perfectly the overall scheme. The title of the display is cut from prepared paper that has been spattered and stamped with matching colours.

Topic ideas

Use nature study to gather detailed drawings and paintings of plants. Use these for all kinds of artwork. Trace some, make repeating patterns to be used for printing on fabric or paper; use Lino with older children. Talk about the ideal world of the Pre-Raphaelites and look at pictures by the Ruralists. Get the children to paint idealised country scenes based on their own drawings, compare these with their work on Lowry's industrial scenery.

Design and make ceramic containers. Use natural shapes as a starting point. Dye some wool using natural materials such as lichen. Use simple card looms to weave with.

Write about the differences between Picasso's and Pre-Raphaelites' portraits.

Resources

Coloured paper, wool, paints, brushes, lichen, photographs, reproduction paintings

Budding Picassos

The display

Picasso's work can be used as a starting point for investigating 2D and 3D space and shapes. The strong colours and distorted portraits in the display are mounted on irregularly spaced tones of beige and browns. The title is an interesting arrangement of cut out black letters.

Topic ideas

Design a questionnaire about Picasso's pictures. How do they make people feel? What colours have been used? Is the style easy to recognise? Include responses in an appreciation gallery (play suitable music).

Try these

Borrow a supermarket trolley and convert it into an animal with one moving part. Take three photographs of a sporting action and convert each into a torn paper shape. Combine these. Make overlapping sketches of faces from different angles, colour them.

Pablo Picasso display
Labelled reproductions and children's interpretations of Picasso's paintings are double mounted and placed on a black background. The oatmeal coloured frieze is about 10 cm wide. Down the centre is a marbled strip in red, white and black.

First Published in 1995 by:
Stanley Thornes (Publishers) Ltd
Ellenborough House
Wellington Street
CHELTENHAM GL50 1YD
England

A catalogue record for this book is available from the British Library.

ISBN 0-7487-1797-8

Printed and bound in Hong Kong by Dah Hua Printing Co., Hong Kong

Typeset by Aetos Ltd; Tadwick, Bath, Avon.